Helion & Company Limited
Unit 8 Amherst Business Centre
Budbrooke Road
Warwick
CV34 5WE
England
Tel. 01926 499 619
Email: info@helion.co.uk
Website: www.helion.co.uk
Twitter: @helionbooks
Visit our blog http://blog.helion.co.uk/

Designed & typeset by Farr out Publications, Wokingham, Berkshire
Cover design Paul Hewitt, Battlefield Design (www.battlefield-design.co.uk)
Printed by Henry Ling Limited, Dorchester, Dorset

ISBN 978-1-912866-34-2

British Library Cataloguing-in-Publication Data
A catalogue record for this book is available from the British Library

We always welcome receiving book proposals from prospective authors.

CONTENTS

Note: In order to simplify the use of this book, all names, locations and geographic designations are as provided in *The Times World Atlas*, or other traditionally accepted major sources of reference, as of the time of described events.

ABBREVIATIONS

AA	Anti-aircraft
AMAS	American Military Assistance Staff
AMG	Allied Military Government
AM	*Aeronautica Militare* (Italian Air Force)
AT	Anti-tank
BETFOR	British Element Trieste Force
DAT	*Difensa Antiaerei Territoriale* (Italian Defence of the Territory)
FSS	Field Security Service
FTT	Free Territory of Trieste
HQ	Headquarters
KNOJ	*Korpus narodne odbrane Jugoslavije* (Yugoslav People's Defence Corps)
JA	*Jugoslovenska armija* (Yugoslav Army)
JNA	*Jugoslovenska Narodna armija* (Yugoslav People's Army)
MAP	Military Assistance Pact
MDAP	Mutual Defence Aid Programme
MZO	*Mešoviti združeni odred* (Mixed Joint Force)
NATO	North Atlantic Treaty Organisation
OZAK	*Operationszone Adriatisches Küstenland* (Operational Zone Adriatic Littoral)
OZNA	*Odeljenje za zaštitu naroda* (Yugoslav Security Service)
QRA	Quick Reaction Alert
RAF	Royal Air Force
SACEUR	Supreme Allied Commander Europe
TRUST	Trieste United States Troops
TSO	Trieste Security Office
VUJA	*Vojna uprava Jugoslovenske armije* (Yugoslav Army Military Government)
UDBA	*Uprava državne bezbednosti* (Yugoslav Department of the State Security)
USAAF	United States Army Air Force
YAF	Yugoslav Air Force

INTRODUCTION

The term "Trieste Crisis" refers to a short but sharp military-political episode in autumn 1953 that was the peak of a much longer conflict over the question of the city of Trieste and the surrounding territory populated by Italians and South Slavs. It was one of the most serious challenges in southern Europe during the early Cold War. Although it started in 1945 and marked the place where the Cold War began, or where "Iron Curtain" ends, the Trieste question would have its conclusion in 1953, when the Italian and Yugoslav Armies massed their troops and nearly ended in open hostilities. Those were the events which shook the stability of the NATO defence against the Soviet bloc threat.

To date there is no one specific monograph that deals with the military side of this issue. One explanation for this lack is the relative unavailability of relevant archival sources in Italy or in former Yugoslavia for many years, and a general focus on other subjects which were treated as much more important. On the contrary, there are a substantial number of available historiographical works which focus on the political, ethnical and other question of the Trieste dispute and we recommend them for further reading; from Jeoffrey Cox (1946) who was the officer in 2nd New Zealand Division; to the works of Jean-Baptiste Duroselle (1966), Bogdan Novak (1970), Roberto G. Rabel (1988), or local authors such as Janko Jeri (1961), Giampaolo Valdevit (1986), Cvetko Vidmar (2009), Bojan Dimitrijević with Dragan Bogetić (2009), up to Miljan Milikić (2012); they have researched the ethnic, political, economic and other aspects of the Trieste problem since 1945.

This book will focus mainly on the military part of the Trieste problem in the period between 1945 and 1954, with emphasis on the "Trieste Crisis", namely: its culmination in 1953 which saw the largest related deployment of the military forces of Italy and Yugoslavia.

The author has researched this matter for many years and was attracted to the subject as this was the most serious military challenge for Tito's Yugoslavia in the Cold War. The author also served as a conscript solider in one of the Yugoslav Army's units in the wider zone of Trieste; although this service was more than thirty years after the events described in this book it added a degree of first-hand experience for a better understanding of the events.

The author has researched in several archives that were situated in Belgrade, as the capital of former Yugoslavia; namely, the Military Archive, Diplomatic Archive of the (Yugoslav) Foreign Ministry and Archive of Yugoslavia as the three most relevant archives for this subject. The other institutions that we have included in our research were the Yugoslav Air Force museum and the Organisational Department of the Serbian Ministry of Defence, since they contained additional organisational facts and figures relating to the Yugoslav forces. The author also had the unique opportunity to research in the *Medija Centar* of the Serbian MoD which has kept extraordinary photo-material of the Yugoslav Army since 1945.

On the other hand, despite some previous contacts the author did not have an opportunity to research in the Italian military archives. However, the work of Filipo Cappellano helped us to understand and describe the role of the Italian military in the crisis. His outstanding study on the activities of the Italian forces formed the basis for our description of the Italian Military involvement. And also, not to forget the *La nuova difesa* web-page, which was very helpful in the reconstruction of the order of battle for the Italian Army during the Trieste Dispute.

The Allied troops, which were garrisoned in Trieste and the surrounding area in 1945-1954 are still missing a good description or detailed monograph, however, the internet pages of the US Army forces (TRUST), as well as the British Army (BETFOR), provided us with adequate tools for outlining the Allied military presence in Trieste – the Free Territory of Trieste.

To avoid the confusion or misinterpretation of the city names and other toponyms in the area, we have used names based on the political allegiance of the locality since 1954. For the places in Italy, the Italian name is given and for those in Yugoslavia (nowadays Slovenia or Croatia) the Slovenian or Croatian version.

1
THE COLD WAR STARTS AT TRIESTE 1945

Yugoslav Partisans and Allies Enter Trieste

> Wholesale [the] Army was fed with the idea that we should liberate Istria and Trieste. When the fighting for Bihać started [...] on all of the lorries and guns were painted slogans: *Forward to Istria, Istria is ours, We shall liberate Trieste,* etc. That was the best proof that the assignment that Marshal Tito had given to the IV Army, reached the mind of every Partisan. Each of the comrades was ready to sacrifice its life, just to fulfil the assignment set out in front of him. For example, when [German] Panthers showed in front of our light tanks, and then the tank crews reported to the Tank Brigade commander, he replied "Trieste or Death!" Generally while XX Division and Tank Brigade advanced to Trieste with the slogan "Trieste or Death![1]

Those words from the report of the Yugoslav Fourth Army after the battle for Trieste was over, on 2-3 May 1945, testified on the military-political intentions of the Yugoslav Partisan/Communist movement led by Josip Broz Tito – perhaps better known as Marshal Tito – and even more: about the enthusiasm and morale which Tito's units had during their advance and while fighting for such an important goal – the city of Trieste.

The city of Trieste stands as a symbol of the Italian-Yugoslav border dispute in the first decade after the Second World War. But the problem included a much larger territory which covers the wider area of Trieste itself. Ranging from Julian Alps in the north to the bottom of the Istrian peninsula, the area where the Italians meet and neighbour the South Slavs. The administrative borders between the states in this area were known and strict but the ethnic divisions over the Julia Region were complex and always a matter of dispute. The prevailing inhabitants in Trieste and other cities of different scale were Italian, while the majority of the rural inhabitants were Slovenes, to the north and around city, and Croats further south in Istria. Simply, the cities were Italian while the peasant land was Slavic. Such division created different views as to who owned the lands. The Italian municipal tradition where cities, no matter their size, were actually the centres of the districts treated the land as Italian in general. The Slovenes and Croats stressed the importance of the territory and lands, perceiving the region as the land settled by Slavs, including the cities, no matter who inhabited them.

In the military sense, the Julian region that surrounds Trieste was a large battlefield in the First World War from 1915-1918 where Italy and Austro-Hungary confronted each other on a massive scale. The belligerence simply replaced the actors in the years between the wars. After the war, in 1918-1919 Italy had moved its borders to the east over former Austro-Hungarian lands covering larger portions of territory inhabited by the South Slavs. On the other side there was Kingdom of Serbs, Croats and Slovenes, later known as the Kingdom of Yugoslavia who stood as the pivot for all South Slavs in South-Eastern Europe. Although with periods of cooperation, Italy and Yugoslavia remained opposed to each other, crowding troops on both sides of the mutual frontier. Italian rule introduced a wave of Italianization over the South Slavs which just added fuel to the poor mutual relations which continued into the Second World War. The turning point was the capitulation of Italy in September 1943.

After the capitulation of Italy, the area that surrounded Trieste including the parts of the Italian province of Friuli (Udine), Italian and Yugoslav pats of Western Slovenia, Istria and parts of the Kvarner

A panorama of Trieste, as caught by a Partisan camera 30 April or 1-2 May 1945. (Military Museum Belgrade)

Partisans of the Yugoslav Fourth Army advancing through the city. (Author's collection)

Stuart tanks of the Yugoslav 1st Tank Brigade seen on the empty Piazza Oberdan and Via Carducci, Trieste, 1 May 1945. (Author's collection)

(Quarnerro) were assembled into a specific German military-administrative organisation titled *Operationszone Adriatisches Küstenland* or simply: OZAK. Collapse of the Italian rule mushroomed the Communist resistance, which at the same time was ethnic, with Slovenes and Croats mostly filling the Partisan ranks. After the two year period of German *bandenkampf* against the Yugoslav Partisans in this area, the fortunes of war changed the path. The Germans and their local collaborators abandoned the historic scene, leaving the previous actors on the edge of the new dispute.

At the end of the Second World War, OZAK became a very important area. For the Germans it was a point of communication between the fronts and a possible area for safe withdrawal from the Balkans or central Italy. For the Allies, advancing from the south and central Italy – an inevitable target where the war had to be finished and bulk of the Axis forces defeated. And finally: for the Yugoslav Partisans – a zone where their national and revolutionary aims would be fulfilled.[2]

On 20 April 1945, the General Staff of the Yugoslav Army ordered its Fourth Army to dash to Trieste, capture the city and continue the advance to the north, following the River Soča (Isonzo) with the intention to cut off the withdrawal of the Wehrmacht's *Heersgruppe E* from the Balkans. One week later, on 27 April, the Fourth Army ordered its 20th Dalmatian Division, with reinforcements and 1st Tank Brigade, to speed-up their advance from the south and to enter Trieste.[3] Tito threw all available forces into the race for Trieste, while leaving sections of Slovenia and Croat territory of Yugoslavia still in German hands.[4]

After the heavy clashes with different German units in the south-east of Trieste, Yugoslav Partisans of the 10th Dalmatian Brigade and 2nd Battalion of the 1st Tank Brigade entered the city on the morning of 1 May and continued fighting against the retreating Germans in the city into the following day, when the first Allied units arrived from the north-west side of the city.[5] These were the spearheads of the XIII Corps of the British Eighth Army and belonged to the 2nd New Zealand Division followed by 6th Armoured Division. In contrast to the Yugoslav Partisans who had fought their way to Trieste since mid-April in clashes all over Dalmatia and the Yugoslav inlands, the Allied troops had advanced to Trieste in the last few days of April, crossing almost 200 kilometres and reaching the Italian cities of Udine, Trieste and Gorizia.[6]

On 2 May the Slovene Partisan forces entered Gorizia and crossed the Isonzo River and met the advancing parties of 2nd New Zealand Division. The New Zealanders proceed to Trieste, and entered the city where Yugoslav Partisans clashed with Germans who desperately wanted to surrender to the Allies, but not to Tito's Partisans. However, clashes continued into the evening of the same day when the last German troops surrendered.[7] On the following day, Germans in the area of the neighbouring village of Opichine would also surrender when the first Allied armoured vehicles approached.

Trieste was liberated, but in the city were two Allied armies with different aims. Tito's propaganda had already claimed that Yugoslav Partisans alone had liberated the city.[8] On 3 May, Yugoslav Partisan HQ created the *Motorizovani odred* (Motorised Detachment) which continued to advance further north following the Isonzo River reaching the Austrian mountain lands.[9]

Tito's Attempts – Allied Strong Response

Once the "Race for Trieste" was over and both the Partisans and the Allies were in the liberated city, an intensive military-diplomatic struggle started. As the Slovene historian Bogdan Novak, pointed out "When British and Yugoslav troops met in Trieste on May 2, 1945 the great problem became: Who would administer the *Julijan* Region?" The Yugoslavs immediately organized their military administration of the city. Prominent Partisan offices of Slovene origin were placed in charge for the city: Josip Černi with Dušan Kveder and Franc Štroka as aides. On the other hand, General Freyberg appointed General Gentry as the commander of all British troops in Trieste on the night between 2 and 3 May.[10]

In some other cases, elsewhere in Yugoslavia during the Second World War, Tito used the policy of *fait accompli* as the basis of establishing of his power.[11] The case of Trieste was much different, however. The city belonged to Italy, and Allied troops appeared immediately after the Partisans and remained in the city. The usual story of "liberation" by the Partisans did not hit the target. Even more, the Italian inhabitants – except for the Communist supporters, showed much more favour to the Allies rather than to Partisans. On the contrary, in the surrounding villages, Slovene inhabitants did not show too much appreciation to the New Zealanders.

Partisans meet New Zealanders of the Sherman equipped A Squadron, 20th Armoured Regiment, 4th Armoured Brigade. (Military Museum Belgrade)

A warm welcome to Tito's Partisans: AEC armoured cars of the 1st Tank Brigade surrounded by Slovene inhabitants. (Author's collection)

The Allies, especially the British, were not impressed with Tito showing off. They started an immediate diplomatic offensive to pull the Yugoslavs out of the city. On the 3 May Tito advised Supreme Allied Commander in Mediterranean, Field Marshal Alexander, that his forces had to withdraw from Zones that the Yugoslav Army had "liberated". Adding that the Allies "appeared… without permission." On the following day, the commander of the 2nd New Zealand Division General Freyberg, also received the same Yugoslav request. Moreover, in the city of Trieste, the Yugoslavs started to act as the only power in charge. They introduced a curfew, partial working obligations, moved the clocks to Yugoslav time and started to make arrests. The first of these arrests brought the notion that the fate of the arrested in some cases was not known after they were taken. It had produced anxiety among the (Italian) citizens, who started to flock around the Allied HQ in the city, complaining of the Yugoslav behaviour and asking for protection.[12]

Tension rose high. More allied troops from British 56th and US 91st divisions reached Trieste and underlined the firm Allied decision not to let Tito's Partisans remain in power over the city.[13] The 56th (London) Division moved up to the Isonzo River and the United States 91st Division took over Gorizia and Palmanova. The British XIII Corps set up their headquarters in Monfalcone. A battalion of American troops from the 363rd Regiment and a battalion of the Scots Guards were brought into Trieste for support. Tensions were now getting strained almost to breaking point and the American battalion and the Scots Guards battalion were withdrawn to their original units and deployed to a 'standby for action' position. The II United States Corps moved up fully on the left of the British XIII Corps along the Isonzo River.[14]

The British Prime Minister was clear in his instructions to Field Marshal Alexander not to negotiate with Tito on any kind of

Daimler armoured cars of the 2nd New Zealand Division, welcomed by the citizens of Gorizia, 3 May 1945. (*Muzej novejše zgodovine Slovenije*, Ljubljana. Hereafter: MNZS)

The 38th (Irish) Brigade's advance towards the old Austro-Yugoslav border did not allow the Yugoslav Motorised Detachment to enter deeper into Italian territory. (Military Museum Belgrade)

annexation of parts of the Italian territory to Yugoslavia. The future of those territories would be dealt with at the peace conference, and Alexander was ordered to clarify this firm Allied standpoint to Tito. On the other side, the Yugoslav communist leader was self-confident in his attempt to take advantage in this matter, but the unexpectedly strong Allied viewpoint and their troops on the ground were something that Tito did not expect. Soon he learned that Stalin and Moscow did not back his movements. Moreover, it provoked disagreements in the communication of the great powers. The lack of Stalin's backing was learned of by the British on 7 May, so they remained firm in preventing Tito's army taking wider actions.[15]

In a way, the temporary division of the troubled area was already on the table, after the talks between Tito and the Allied delegation headed by British Lieutenant General William Morgan, Chief of Staff to Field Marshall Alexander, on 8 May 1945 in Belgrade. Morgan produced a map with the division of the Julia region which would later be known as the "Morgan Line." The agreement was on hold for almost a month. But after Tito discovered the lack of Moscow's support and felt the pressure by the Allies on the ground he became more open for acceptance of the proposed temporary division of the territories. In the meantime he ordered the withdrawal of Partisan forces which were west of the Isonzo/Soča River, as General Morgan asked for upon leaving Belgrade on 10 May.[16] The Yugoslav General Staff ordered on 20 May that Partisan forces should withdraw from Slovene inhabited parts of Furlania and remain on the left bank of Isonzo/Soča River. It was a considerable shock for the Slovene Partisans who expected that those parts should become part of the New Yugoslavia/Slovenia. Slovene Partisan forces abandoned the cities of Udine, Cividale, Gemona and Tarcento up to 23 May 1945.[17]

Around Trieste and further south, however, the situation was different. As Italian historian Giampoalo Valdevit suggests the "overlapping" of the Allied and Yugoslav Army zones, was the core problem.[18] The Allies wanted to avoid any clash with Tito's Yugoslavs, their war-time allies, a point that is vividly clear from the communication between Prime Minister Churchill and US President Truman between 14-16 May 1945. On the ground, the tension between yesterday's allies grew. The Partisans started to dislike the Allies as they were seen as an obstacle to their aims. The Allied troops became aware of numerous misconducts against civilians and political opponents made by the Partisans in the area, which corrupted their earlier admiration.[19] Geoffrey Cox, an intelligence officer of the New Zealand Division describes Partisan rule in the city as "that of the iron hand." Bogdan Novak, explains that the Partisan's usage of the term "fascism" or "fascist" signified every potential opponent to communism. Knowing that fact, the "Yugoslav persecutions in the Julian region can be better understood."[20]

Upon President Truman's instruction, the Allies were ordered to make a show of force in a march manoeuvre between Trieste and Gorizia. Most likely with the same intentions, Tito ordered that the Yugoslav 2nd Tank Brigade, with Soviet T-34 tanks, move on 17 May from Zagreb and march all the way to Trieste. Yugoslav tanks rolled through Trieste's streets on 21 May, demonstrating the Yugoslav Partisans' power and settled in the nearby Vipava valley, some 25 kilometres from the city.[21] Tito counted that both of his tank brigades, with other Partisan divisions gathered around the city, would impress the Allies and be the trump for the political conquest of Trieste. On the next two days, Eighth Army forces carried out demonstrative movements between Trieste and Gorizia. Truman's standpoint that if "our demonstration of force should be full-scale, some kind of agreement will be achieved" was right.[22] On the following day, the Yugoslavs accepted negotiations. These started in Belgrade on 25 May and finished on 9 June with agreement on a temporary military government in Julia region/Slovene Littoral and the city of Pula.[23]

As Rabel suggests, the "Trieste imbroglio" represented the first case of direct East-West military confrontation faced by the Truman administration. Tito's actions were perceived as communist aggression and they convinced Truman of the efficacy of a firm but restrained response.[24] As the chief of the US military mission to Yugoslavia in 1945, Colonel Franklin Lindsay, concludes: the "First face-to-face East-West confrontation, which was to grow into the Cold War, began in Trieste."[25]

Same place – different armies: Armoured and other vehicles of the 2nd New Zealand Division (MNZS Ljubljana) and units of Yugoslav Fourth Army at main square in Trieste. (Military Museum Belgrade)

Withdrawal of the Yugoslav forces and Allied Temporary Administration

For an understanding of the whole Trieste problem, one point is particularity crucial, made also by Franklin Lindsay: "the Yugoslavs had convinced themselves that they had become the co-equal of the United States, Britain and the Soviet Union… In my subsequent talks with the partisans they asserted they had earned [the] right to sit at the same table as the Big Three and to participate fully in post-war territorial arrangements." On the other side, as Lindsay points out: "the Allies still regarded the partisans as a band of irregulars who had made a useful but peripheral contribution in a backwater theatre of the war… It was a shock to each side to find how different the other's perceptions were."[26]

By the agreement signed in Belgrade between the Allies and Yugoslavia on the 9 June 1945, a temporary Allied Military Government (AMG – actually the HQ of the British XIII Corps) was set up in Trieste and the surrounding territory. The main negotiators, General Morgan and Yugoslav General Arso Jovanović, Yugoslav Chief of Staff, met in Duino Castle.[27]

The Morgan-Jovanović Agreement divided the disputed territory

Pro-Yugoslav and pro-communist demonstrations in the Trieste, mid-May 1945. (Military Museum Belgrade)

Post-card issued by the Yugoslavs in May 1945 with the clear message: "Tito's Army liberated Trieste." (Aleksandar Smiljanić collection)

A column of Sherman tanks belonging to the 20th Armoured Regiment, 4th Armoured Brigade, 2nd New Zealand Division, parked in one of the main streets of Trieste. (MNZS Ljubljana)

of Venezia Julia into following zones:

- Zone A, consisted of Trieste, Gorizia and the surrounding area, including the city of Pula with Allied forces and the Yugoslav *odred* that was under the command of the British XIII Corps.
- Zone B, north-western Istria, the Slovenian Littoral, Rijeka and Kvarner with Yugoslav forces.

Each of Zones was to be administered by the respective Military Governments until a final settlement had been reached in the peace treaties that were to follow.

Article 2 restricted the size of the Yugoslav Army in Zone A to a regular force of 2,000 men including all ranks, the Yugoslav unit was allocated a certain territory which would be designated by the Supreme Allied Commander, and logistics for the Yugoslav troops were taken over by the Allied force. Under Article 3, a "small" Yugoslav mission would be attached to the British Eighth Army as observers. All other Yugoslav Army forces should withdraw. It was ordered that Yugoslav troops moved to the demarcation line, ranging from north to south: Mangrt – Sveta Gora – Komen – Veliko Gradišče – Golič – the valley of the Glinščica River – Miljski Hribi – Debeli Rtič, on the 12 June at 0800 hours GMT. This line was nicknamed Morgan's Line.[28]

Yugoslav forces started movement even before the agreed date. During 11 June they started to abandon the designated area.[29] "When the *Jugoslavs* withdrew to Zone B they did so in good order. Their flag over the Town Hall was replaced by the Union flag and the Stars and Stripes," later remembered Douglas Lyle, of British 21st Port Security Section.[30]

The word that the Yugoslav troops would withdraw spread on the 9 June. It caused hesitation and a decline of morale within the units that took part in the previous combat on the way to Trieste such as the 3rd Dalmatian Brigade of the 9th Dalmatian Division which was ordered to move to the east into Srem.[31] The 43rd Division went to Maribor. Other units such as the 19th and 26th Dalmatian divisions took positions in the wider Western Slovenia or Istria. Movement of other forces in the wider area continued during the following days of June. The Yugoslav 1st Tank Brigade, with Stuart light tanks, went to Vrhnika near Ljubljana, while the 2nd – with Soviet T-34s, was sent to Macedonia.[32]

The force of 2,000 men remained in Zone A as the *Odred* formed by the HQ of 20th Dalmatian Division and the men assembled from 9th, 20th and 26th Dalmatian, 43rd Istrian and Slovene Peoples Defence divisions, combined with an artillery battalion from the Fourth Army and a tank company from 1st Tank Brigade.[33] After the *Odred* was assembled in Trieste, the last of the Yugoslav 20th Division abandoned the city. All of the establishments and symbols of the Yugoslav (Communist) government were erased following the Allied Military Government decision on 24 June. This was a necessary step to prevent all Yugoslav illegal activities which may remain.[34] "When AMG took charge of the Government, the Government that had existed here under the *Jugoslavs* merely moved into another headquarters. From the first the Slavs adopted an attitude of non-cooperation with AMG, and a Communist dominated shadow government of the Slavs continued to attempt to dictate to the Slavic population."[35]

Following the articles of the agreement, the Allied force organized a reconnaissance party which headed for city of Pula, at the bottom of the Istrian peninsula, on 16 June. The Yugoslav Army was responsible for escorting those troops. In following days the Allied force took over the positions in this important Adriatic harbour.[36]

As Croatian diplomat Mario Mikolić wrote in his study: "contrary to Italian historians, we can say that this division of territories was closest to actual ethnical boundaries. Maybe, Slovenia lost a bit more. But it did not match the geostrategic, political or economic interests

T-34/85s of the Yugoslav 2nd Tank Brigade roll into Trieste on 21 May 1945. (Military Museum Belgrade)

General Morgan inspecting Yugoslav troops in the vicinity of Trieste. (Vasil Micevski collection)

Slovene Partisan unit on the move in Trieste. (Military Museum Belgrade)

A tank company from the 1st Tank Brigade remained in the *Odred*. Here an AA modified Stuart adorned with different slogans and the symbol of the *Odred* on the side of the tank. (Mario Raguž collection)

of either of the sides. It was one of the most absurd compromises which did not result in [a] long lasting solution."[37] It would be a short division and would last only two years.

According to the agreement signed on 9 June 1945, the Yugoslav Partisan presence in the city of Trieste was over. Many contemporaries commented that ruthless behaviour, arrests and several hundred victims of Tito's security service purges, actually turned the city against its Slavic liberators. A Croatian politician *émigré* Bogdan Radica wrote what he have heard in those days in the disputed area: "wherever the Englishmen arrived, there is food, freedom is absolute and people accept them with sympathy."[38]

Creation of the Yugoslav and Allied Military Governments

After the withdrawal of the Yugoslav forces was carried out, Yugoslav and Allied representatives continued the negotiations between 13 and 20 June in the HQ of the British XIII Corps, situated in a fortress north of Trieste. The questions which remained for discussion were: disposition of the Yugoslav force within the Allied Military Government, composition and responsibilities of the Yugoslav mission with the British Eighth Army, civil authorities under the AMG, war booty captured by the Yugoslav forces and movement of the civil inhabitants. Difficult talks finally came to an agreement on 20 June.[39]

In line with this agreement, the Yugoslav *Odred* would concentrate in Zone A, north of Trieste in the area: M. Tersteli (Trstelj) – Suta – Vonssizza – Opacchiasella (Opatje selo) – Coll Grande (Veliki Hrib) – M. Terstel. It was specified that the *Odred* would be under Allied logistics, except for weapons, ammunition and vehicles. In the chain of command it was subordinated to the Allied HQ which was ordered to contact the Yugoslav Army on behalf of the *Odred*.[40]

Initially, the *Odred* included the units stationed in Gorizia and Pula, headquartered in the village of Repentabor near Sežana but after the agreement was made it was transferred to a designated zone with an HQ in the village of Kostajnevica at Kras (Carso), south from Gorizia overlooking the link from Trieste to Monfalcone. Later the Yugoslav *Odred* spread its area of responsibility all over Kras, from the Vipava River to the north to the villages above Trieste to the south. Its HQ moved from Kostanjevica to nearby Opatje Selo on 4 September 1945 and remained there until 15 September 1947. The *Odred* was commanded by the Slovene Partisan Colonel Dragomir Benčić. Later, in turn 1945/46, the initial personnel of the *Odred* were replaced by the troops of the 26th Dalmatian Division.[41]

The Yugoslav Army mission with the Eighth Army was commanded by Colonel Rado Pehaček, a distinguished Slovene partisan, and later general and head of the Yugoslav military intelligence in the 1950s. It was located in the village of Aurisina (Nabrežina) which was in the middle of the road between Trieste and the HQ of XIII Corps.[42] The agreement of Duino specified mission personnel and the responsibilities in assisting the *Odred*, Yugoslav Army and Government. From the Yugoslav side, this mission was responsible to the II Intelligence Department of the Yugoslav General Staff and it remained operational until 1946. Finally, control of the troop movements was also agreed, and all of the war booty in the area was confirmed as Yugoslav property. Activities for gathering the war booty were run by the commission which existed in Trieste during 1945; it was manned mostly by Yugoslav intelligence officers, but also carefully monitored by the Allies' security.[43]

In Zone B on 25 June 1945, the Yugoslavs created their own military government known by the abbreviation VUJA (*Vojna uprava Jugoslovenske armije*). It was responsible for all military–civil

Members of the *Odred* posing for the camera, while a British military policeman is clearly seen in the background. (M. Raguž collection)

issues in Zone. The Yugoslav military administration had direct control over customs, traffic, finances, prices, and over the management of the larger industrial and mining enterprises. It was also supreme judicial authority. The commander of the VUJA was directly responsible to and received orders from the Yugoslav Government.[44] The first commander was General Petar Drapšin, previous commander of the IV Army, but he was soon replaced by General Vječeslav Holjevac, later much better known as the mayor of the city of Zagreb. Regular Yugoslav Army troops from 7th, 20th, and 26th divisions were stationed elsewhere in Zone.[45] A local para-military organisation, *Narodna zaštita,* was also formedwithin Zone, acting as the auxiliary force for the Yugoslav Security Service (OZNA). The OZNA HQ for the "Slovene" part of Zone was established in Ajdovščina.[46]

After the Yugoslav evacuation, the Allied Military Government (AMG) was set up in Trieste on 12 June and in Gorizia two days later. It is interesting to note that the AMG for the Julian Region set up its HQ at Udine on 22 May and readied provincial teams for Trieste and Gorizia provinces, pending the outcome of negotiations with Marshal Tito. The Trieste team entered that city on 25 May under strict orders not to disclose their identity as military government officers.[47]

The acting commander of the AMG was Colonel Nelson Monfort. He was subordinated to the General Harding (commander of the XIII Corps). Monfort was soon to be replaced by the US Colonel Alfred Connor Bowman from 4 July 1945, and Bowman was replaced by Colonel James Carnes on 25 June 1947. The Allied forces stationed in the disputed area remained under the responsibility of the General Harding's XIII Corps and included US and British forces. The units which were deployed after the war (10th Indian Infantry Division and

Table 1. British battalions deployed in the Triest and Pula regions 1945-1947

Battalion	Dates	Location
2nd Coldstream Guards	May 1945 – May 1946	Rossetti barracks
1st Scots Guards	May 1945 – May 1946	Rossetti barracks
1st London Irish Rifles	May 1945 – December 1946	Rossetti barracks
1st London Scottish	May 1945 – December 1946	Rossetti barracks
1st King's Own Regiment	May 1945 – May 1950	Rossetti barracks
2nd Queen's Own Cameron Highlanders	August 46 – March 47	Rossetti barracks
1st Ox & Bucks Light Infantry	May 1947	Rossetti barracks
1st Worcester Regiment (part)	August 1946 – May 1947	Rossetti barracks
7th North Staffordshire Regiment	November 1945 – August 1946	Lazzaretto barracks
4th Dorset Regiment	April 1946 – September 1946	Lazzaretto barracks
Royal Northumberland Fusiliers	April 1946 – September 1946	Lazzaretto barracks
2nd Essex Regiment	August 1946 – May 1947	Lazzaretto barracks
1st Border Regiment	October 1946 – March 1947	Lazzaretto barracks
1st Royal Sussex Regiment	April 1946 – June 1947	Sistina/Opicina
1st Welch Regiment	April 1946 – June 1947	Sistina/Opicina
9th Royal Fusiliers	May 1945 – December 1946	Pula
2nd Monmouthshire Regt	March 1946 – September 1946	Pula
1st Worcester Regiment (part)	August 1946 – May 1947	Pula

Yugoslav infantry belonging to the 26th Dalmatian Division, seen at Ilirska Bistrica barracks in 1946. (Military Museum Belgrade)

the US Army's 34th Infantry Division) remained during the summer of 1945. In the autumn, they were replaced by the US Army's 88th Infantry Division, commanded by General Bryand Moore, which took over some units and personnel of the 34th Division. The British forces were subordinated to the 56th (London) Infantry Division, also a veteran force from the Italian campaign, commanded by General Whitfield. It remained in the area until its disbandment in the summer of 1946. The Americans were deployed in the northern part of the Morgan Line, from Predel at the Austrian border all over the Gorizia region to Dornberk – a village and railway junction at the Vipava River, south east from Gorizia. The British forces controlled the southern part of Morgan's Line from Dornberk to Debeli Rtič (at the west side of the Trieste bay) and the city of Pula. Both forces had garrisons in the city of Trieste.[48]

The British Army deployed battalions on a rotational basis to Triest and Pula in the period between 1945 and 1947.

In addition to the infantry battalions listed in Table 1, the British Army also deployed elements of the appropriate support services and branches.[49]

Table 2. British intelligence and security detachments 1945-1946[50]

Unit	Duties	Location
21 Port Security Section	general counter-intelligence duties	Trieste
412 FSS	general counter-intelligence duties	Trieste
414 FSS	vetting for the AMG	Trieste
35 FSS		Monfalcone
12 FSS		Gorizia
419 FSS		Udine
411 FSS		Udine
5 Special Counter-Intelligence Unit		Trieste
Censorship Group		Trieste
CSDIC Detachment		Trieste

In addition to the above units there were four other sections to the north.

Incidents in 1946: The Shooting Down of Two USAAF Aircraft

New tensions in the territory surrounding Trieste occurred in November 1945. Some 8,000 troops of the II Polish Corps, commanded by General Wladyslaw Anders, arrived in the city of Udine. During December 1945, 700 of the Polish troops were seen in Trieste "without markings." Concentration of the Polish forces continued in January 1946, which expanded into February 1946, when the whole of General Anders' force was concentrated in the area between Bologna – Rimini – Padova – Venice – Treviso – Udine. In Trieste, rumours were heard that the Poles would replace the US 88th Infantry Division which was located in Zone A.[51] The Yugoslavs were sensitive to the presence of Anders' force, manned by anti-communist veterans who refused to return to Poland. They posed a serious danger to the Yugoslav communist government in the area, since they may have become popular with the Slovene inhabitants, by being Slavic, Catholic, and anti-communist. The Poles always looked carefully for exiled Royal Yugoslav troops in Italy who had been treated as enemies by Tito's Yugoslavia. In addition, they amounted to a force of almost 100,000 veteran-troops, which outmatched the Yugoslav military capacities in the western parts of Yugoslavia.

From the beginning of January, Yugoslav units carried out "minimal" movements in response to the appearance of the Polish forces. The Yugoslav authorities officially denied such activities stressing that their troops were partly demobilised on 1 January 1946, and reorganized on 1 March 1946. They had rejected the Allied accusations by stressing that the number of the deployed divisions was not an indication of the total number of the Yugoslav forces in the area. On the other side, the Yugoslavs accused the Allies of an increase in the number of provocations on the borders, violations of their air space, the insertion of terrorist anti-communist groups and the deployment of II Polish Corps.[52]

Although the Yugoslavs officially denied the redeployment of their troops towards Trieste and Italy, the preserved documentation showed that they actually strengthened their forces. The 2nd Tank Brigade was rushed from Macedonia between 8 and 14 February, reaching the city of Logatec, on the Ljubljana – Trieste road between 12 and 17 February. The other tank brigade, the 1st from Vrhnika, left its barracks on 9 February moving closer to the border.[53] The usage of armoured units was always a sign of serious intention in the Yugoslav military circles. Both of the brigades joined the 1st Tank Division with its HQ set up in Kranj.

The Yugoslav 28th Division was moved from its garrisons in Croatia to Western Slovenia on the 23 February. During the night of 26-27 February its 21st Slavonian Brigade entered Zone B and was stationed in the city of Pazin in the middle of Istrian peninsula. It

Yugoslavia returns the bodies of the USAAF C-47 crew that were shot down on 19 August 1946 at the demarcation line between the two zones. (Tomaž Perme collection)

was subordinated to the 26th Division which was at the time responsible for the garrisons in Zone B as well as the *Odred* in Zone A.[54] In the same period, the 2nd Mixed Aviation Division in Zagreb despatched its 422nd Assault Aviation Regiment (Il-2 Shturmoviks) to Cerklje air base, while the 113th Fighter Regiment (Yak fighters) in Ljubljana was alerted to adopt a higher combat readiness.[55] Yugoslav sources claimed 233 violations of the Yugoslav air space between 11 February and 26 March 1946.[56]

Those tensions complicated the relations with the Allies on the political level. Yugoslav diplomats explained that those movements were not against the Allied forces in Trieste and the wider area, but were intended to "prevent possible provocations which were [a] threat to us, and came from different pro-fascist elements and especially from Polish troops of General Anders, which mobilised former *Ustashi* and *Chetniks*."[57]

Again in the summer of 1946, tensions rose. Movements were frequent from both sides of the border. The Yugoslavs complained about the movements of the British 56th Infantry Division in June and July. Actually, this division and the 6th Armoured Division were moved from the area after the ceremony in the Trieste but the "number of the perimeters and military tents alongside of the Morgan Line continued to grow". The Yugoslavs noted the appearance of Allied warships in Trieste harbour, as well as armed anti-communist Yugoslav groups crossing the border. The Yugoslavs counted numerous airspace violations. The most serious incident occurred on the evening of 12 July 1946, at the village of Krm near Kobarid. Both sides blamed the other for being responsible for the incident, but it remains a fact that American soldiers of the 88th Division were in the village, deep in the territory controlled by the Yugoslav forces, and that they opened fire killing two Yugoslav soldiers. In the Yugoslav diplomatic note the Allies were accused of having tolerated "systematic assaults of the mob on the Yugoslav Army members in Trieste." There were a couple of such incidents and even the political commissioner of the Yugoslav *Odred* and his aides were attacked in Gorizia on 9 August. Yugoslav diplomats made the accusation that the AMG's officers took part in such incidents together with the "fascist mob" pointing out that the attackers were the same people who had waged the war against the Allies just last year.[58]

In fact, there were many violations of Yugoslav airspace in the border areas in the first half of the 1946. Yugoslavs pretentiously counted them and reacted through diplomatic channels. The most serious incident occurred in August 1946 when Yugoslav fighters shot down two USAAF transport aircraft. It would add a serious burden to diplomatic relations between the United States and Yugoslavia for several years ahead.

What was actually the problem? Allied air forces in northern Italy maintained communication with their other units based in Austria. In many cases, Allied pilots were reluctant to take care over the boundaries of Yugoslavian air space, since it was treated as an allied country, and so they flew directly from Treviso or Udine to Klagenfurt or Vienna. On the other side, the Yugoslav military top brass decided to stop those intrusions and to react firmly. The HQ of the Yugoslav Air Force ordered the movement of the 3rd Fighter Division from Mostar via Novi Sad to Ljubljana airfield. The division reached Ljubljana on the 1 July 1946. It was equipped with two fighter regiments with Soviet Yak fighters, which established a fighter pair at combat readiness No.1.[59]

There were several Yugoslav attempts to intercept the Allied planes during July but without success. At 12:50 p.m. on 9 August, a pair of Yak fighters shot down a USAAF C-47 en route from Vienna to Udine, in the area between Ljubljana and Kranj. The crew and several passengers survived a crash landing with minor injuries. Ten days after, on the 19 August, a Yugoslav fighter pair taking off from an ambush set up in Radovljica, shot down another C-47 at 1007 hrs. All members of the crew on board were killed in the incident.[60]

The Americans were furious. US Ambassador Patterson in Belgrade bitterly said to Marshal Tito: "One and a half years ago, you had welcomed our airplanes. Now you are shooting them down! My Government find this treatment of the airplanes belonging to a friendly country as totally inappropriate. This doing will create [a] deep impression in the minds of the American people…"[61] Half a month later, Tito agreed to pay compensation to the families of the dead US airmen and promised that there would be firing on Allied airplanes if they were caught in Yugoslav air space, though Tito stressed to the US ambassador that "we have rights to protect sovereignty."[62]

These two incidents did not prevent Allied aircraft from using the short-cut over Yugoslavia or from violating Yugoslav air space later in the 1946, but they did raise tensions in the relations between Tito's Yugoslavia and the Allies.[63] This incident actually showed the radical attitude towards the West that Tito and his disciples in Belgrade had during this period and appeared to be much more radical than its mentors in Moscow. It also complicated the situation over Trieste, since it brought up further mistrust in Yugoslav-Allied relations.

On 9 September 1946, US military police disarmed two groups of Yugoslav soldiers, with one captain and ten soldiers, who were sent into the city to take over some UNRRA materials. In the turn of 1946-1947 other incidents continued to spoil mutual relations. They occurred mostly at checkpoints of both sides; soldiers were lost on both sides, and there were scuffles with the locals and other similar incidents. Yugoslav authorities mostly complained of the anti-communist (Yugoslav) groups which illegally commuted over the borders.[64]

The conclusion for this list of incidents was that the Morgan Line "increasingly becomes a boundary harder to cross than any frontier with Western countries. It was rapidly turning into an iron curtain dividing two systems of life", as Bogdan Novak suggests.[65]

2
ESTABLISHING THE FREE TERRITORY OF TRIESTE 1947

New Zonal Division

A new stage in the Trieste issue arrived in 1947. The Free Territory of Trieste was formed at the peace conference in Paris. On the basis of Article 21 of the protocol of the Peace Treaty with Italy, the Free Territory of Trieste was formed. It would be known with the abbreviation FTT, STT (in Serbo-Croatian: *Slobodna Teritorija Trsta*), STO (Slovenian: *Svobodno Trzasko Ozemlje*) or TLT (Italian: *Territorio Libere di Trieste*).[1] Yugoslavia accepted the creation of the FTT, but stated that it do not give up its "rightful" territorial claims.

The Free Territory of Trieste was created at the Peace Treaty in February 1947, but with an effective start date on 15 September 1947 when the treaty was ratified "by the Big Four Powers, United States, Great Britain, France and USSR."[2] The division between Yugoslavia and Italy would also be effective from the same night of 15-16 September 1947.

The territory of the FTT was divided in two zones: A and B, not to be confused with the earlier Zones A and B. The core of the new Zone A was the city of Trieste with a narrow coastal strip to the north-west. Zone B was larger and created from the territory south from Trieste in the north-western part of the Istrian peninsula.[3]

This free state never achieved the planned self-government, and remained under two military governments: the Allied and the Yugoslav. Elections for the local municipalities would be held twice, in 1949 and 1952, but there were no elections for the FTT Assembly. It may thus be concluded that the FTT was never a real independent state but rather a kind of provisorium. The official languages were Italian and Slovenian with the provision of Serbo-Croatian in the southern communities in Zone B. Most of the Italians lived in the city of Trieste and other minor cities while Slovenes and Croats dominated in the rural settlements. The figures on the population differ, since the Yugoslavs always downplayed the number of Italian inhabitants in Zone B.[4]

The Allied troops were in Zone A, while the Yugoslav troops were obliged to move into Zone B when the division and redeployment came in mid-September 1947. The FTT were allowed 5,000 troops while the rest of the Yugoslav and Allied forces were supposed to move deeper into Italian or Yugoslav territory.[5]

The news about the reorganisation of Zones and areas of responsibilities reached General Ante Banina, the commander of the Yugoslav *odred* in Zone A in spring 1947. He had sent one of his aides, an officer from the 1st Proletarian Brigade, to Allied HQ to express complaints about the new zones.[6] It illustrated the fact that the Yugoslav military commanders on the ground did not have adequate information on the higher Yugoslav diplomatic and political standpoints which they had to follow and that this sometimes produced problems.

In the autumn of 1946, the Yugoslav Army sent its elite 1st Proletarian Division to Postojna with the intention of reinforcing the Yugoslav forces that surrounded Trieste. In March 1947, the 1st Proletarian Brigade of the 1st Proletarian Division, considered to be the most elite of the Yugoslav formations, took over responsibility in Zone A with the US Army's 88th Infantry Division. The complete brigade now acted as the Yugoslav Army *Odred* in Zone A. It was deployed in the area between Trieste and Gorizia, while maintaining one company in Trieste, and the hospital in Gorizia, where the HQ of the 88th Division was. The task was difficult: "It had to adapt and live together with Anglo-American units." Allied officers were attached to the Brigade HQ. The Yugoslavs decided to

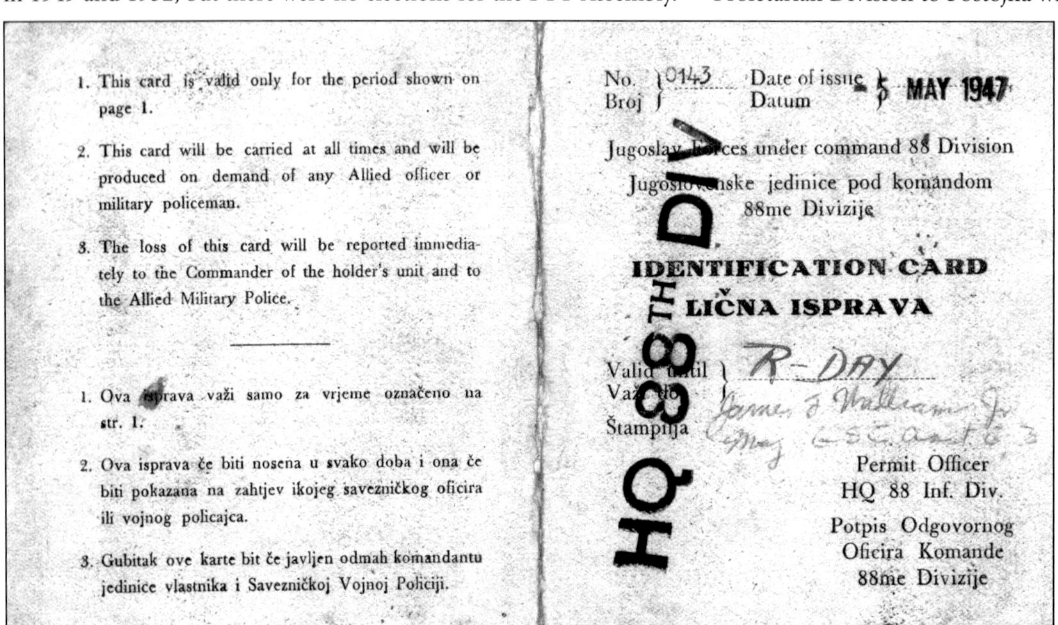
1. This card is valid only for the period shown on page 1.
2. This card will be carried at all times and will be produced on demand of any Allied officer or military policeman.
3. The loss of this card will be reported immediately to the Commander of the holder's unit and to the Allied Military Police.

1. Ova isprava važi samo za vrjeme označeno na str. 1.
2. Ova isprava će biti nosena u svako doba i ona će biti pokazana na zahtjev ikojeg savezničkog oficira ili vojnog policajca.
3. Gubitak ove karte bit će javljen odmah komandantu jedinice vlastnika i Savezničkoj Vojnoj Policiji.

No. / Broj 0143 Date of issue / Datum 5 MAY 1947

Jugoslav Forces under command 88 Division
Jugoslovenske jedinice pod komandom 88me Divizije

HQ 88TH DIV

IDENTIFICATION CARD
LIČNA ISPRAVA

Valid until / Važi do R-DAY

Štampilja

Permit Officer
HQ 88 Inf. Div.
Potpis Odgovornog Oficira Komande 88me Divizije

Identification card of the soldiers belonging to the Yugoslav *odred*, valid from 5 May 1947 to R-Day or Ratification Day, 16 September 1947. (David Orlović collection)

"And You Allies, respect our wishes" graffiti at the edge of the two zones, 1947. (*Medija Centar Odbrana*, further as MCO)

keep the real name of the unit secret, as in Soviet practice, and naively answered that the name of the unit was actually "*odred*." Soon after the deployment, the brigade/*odred* was inspected by General Moore, the commander of the 88th Division, and greeted the Yugoslav commander and brigade staff with the unit's real name. Tito's officers were surprised that the Allies were so well informed. Yugoslav Communist self-confidence was enormous and sometimes difficult in contact with their Allied colleagues. Such attitude of former victorious Partisans, now peace-time regular soldiers, was maybe crucial in understanding of the Trieste crisis in general. Tito's forces overlooked not just the Italians but even the Allies as a fighting force. Moreover, they thought that control over Trieste was justified by their victory over other local factions in the Second World War.[7]

During the same month, 1st Tank Brigade from Vrhnika detached one tank battalion with Stuart tanks and, with additional men from the 1st Tank Division, created the Motomechanized Regiment on 17 March 1947 and was dubbed as the "Yugoslav *odred* in Zone B". The regiment reached Zone B between 29 April and 1 May and settled in Koper and the surrounding villages of Dekani and Valdaltre – at the edge of the Zone and almost overlooking Trieste.[8] It was an important sign – the Yugoslavs had placed their tanks almost in the suburbs of the city.

The reinforcements were an indication that the Yugoslavs intended to strengthen their forces around the disputed areas in the period after the peace conference in Paris and especially during the peace negotiations and expected favourable treatment of Italy by the Allies. But soon after the Yugoslavs realized that the division of the territories would take place in mid-September they became suspicious and impatient. On 13 September Yugoslav forces moved closer to the new borders; the 1st Tank Brigade reached Dolnje Jezero near Cerknica on the pre-war Italian – Yugoslav border, waiting for further orders.[9]

Tension with the Allies rose, while the riots and incidents in the city of Trieste just increased the Yugoslav impatience. The commander of the IV Army, responsible for the operation from the Yugoslav side, sent a telegram to General Airey, arrogantly urging that the withdrawal of the Allied force into the new boundaries should be carried out immediately. The intention was that the Yugoslav Army should take control over the new borders in the first hours of 16 September.[10] This would be "R" Day.

Finally, Yugoslav forces moved towards the new frontiers on the night of 15-16 September 1947. Colonel Pehaček, now as the chief of the Yugoslav mission with the British XIII Corps HQ, received an order directly from Tito. Pehaček was ordered to inform the commander of the corps that the Yugoslav forces had been ordered to take control over the territories, from 00:00 a.m. hours on the 16 September. The British commander was irritated with such behaviour of the Yugoslav Army and the Allied forces generally did not hurry and continued to prepare for withdrawal step by step. After many strong words, it was decided that one British staff officer should accompany Colonel Pehaček to Ajdovščina, where the temporary Yugoslav HQ was located, to avoid any misunderstandings. As their automobile met motorised columns of the Yugoslav Army loaded with soldiers carrying full armament and heading towards the new Yugoslav frontiers, Pehaček remembered the British officer turned pale and just observed the movements without words. Following this Yugoslav pressure, Allied HQ ordered that their forces should abandon the area, which they did in a hurry, up until midnight of 16 September. They moved later deeper into Italian territory.[11]

A reporter from the Yugoslav army magazine *Front* followed one motorised column which had the task of reaching the new northern border of Yugoslavia that night. At 00:00 a.m. hours of the 16 September – "R" Day, Yugoslav forces passed the earlier demarcation line and entered into the "new" territories in the North Primorska area passing Most-na-Soči, Volče, Idrsko and Mlinsko. The column reached Kobarid at 00:45 a.m., which had been abandoned by US troops. The motorised column proceeded through Trnova and Dvor to Bovec, where the vehicles were halted by the cheering Slovene population, even though it was at night. From Bovec, this motorised unit moved to Predile where a new border crossing was established.[12] Air cover for the whole operation between 16 and 18 September was provided by eight Yak fighters from the 112th and 254th Fighter Regiment at Ljubljana – Polje airfield.[13]

Odred JA was redeployed from the earlier Zone A to Zone B retaining the same units, and an incident occurred during this movement. The *Odred* was based near Opatje Selo and its HQ decided not to move through Yugoslav territory but to take the shortest route – through the new Zone A. The *Odred* moved to the shore with the intention of passing through Trieste and crossing into the new Zone B. Seeing the column of vehicles and tanks, the Allies concluded that the Yugoslavs were heading for Trieste and halted the Yugoslavs and threatened to open fire on the column. After a short debate on the road, the *odred*'s HQ decided to continue their movement on the Yugoslav side. The *odred* reached the city of Portorož in Zone B later the same day.[14]

This event was described by Franklin Lindsay, who points that one US Army sergeant allegedly stopped Yugoslav *odred*:

"Shortly after midnight a Yugoslav tank column rumbled up to an isolated checkpoint in the hills behind Trieste that marked [the] boundary of the Allied Zone… The Yugoslav officer in the lead tank

Yugoslav forces enter Pula, 16 September 1947. (MCO)

Training in the 1st Proletarian Rifle Regiment, Dekani near Koper, 1948. (MCO)

ordered the sergeant to stand aside to let the column enter the Zone. The sergeant refused and calmly set up his machine gun on its tripod in the centre of the road, pointing at the tank. He then sat down behind it, telling the Yugoslav officer his orders were to let no one pass and he intended to do just that. Meanwhile he radioed for support."

Lindsay concludes that without the intervention of this sergeant, the Yugoslav forces would have carried out an "unopposed sneak" into Zone A, which would later make it "far harder" to take them out.[15] However, it was the only incident in this territory exchange between Yugoslavs and Allies which was finished by 16:00 p.m. hours of the 16 September 1947.[16]

The official history of the US Army's 351st Regiment comments upon the role of the unit at that time, which also attribute the following words to Lindsay:

> In the days of covering the Ratification of the Italian Peace Treaty, the 351st Infantry, though its ranks thinned by redeployment and with inexperienced troops being sent from Zone of Interior, with small numbers of combat tried men, again demonstrated to the whole world that they were ready for whatever confronted them and their actions were of a superior kind in some of the more serious incidents arising from misunderstanding between the *Jugoslav* FTT Force and Zone A [British and United States] Forces. Officers and men of the 351st Infantry, in performing their duties on "R" Day, showed aggressive spirit, initiative, superior conduct and devotion to duty, which also demonstrated their superior training spirit and morale.[17]

On the same night of 15 – 16 September, Yugoslav forces also entered the city of Pula at the southern point of the Istrian Peninsula. Yugoslav Army officials there complained that the American forces in Pula had demolished and destroyed some of the properties that were to be passed to the Yugoslav authorities. The Yugoslav Naval Command of the Northern Adriatic moved from the city of Rijeka, soon followed by the two naval schools which would form the Naval NCO School in Pula.[18] Much later, on 8 March 1948, the 112th Fighter Regiment from Ljubljana-Polje arrived at the abandoned Allied air base near Pula and took over the air defence of this part of Yugoslavia.[19]

Cadets of the Reserve Infantry Officers School, "Southern Barracks", Vipava 1951. (MCO)

First Platoon of the Machine Gun Company, 2nd Battalion of the 106th Infantry Regiment, 1st Proletarian Division, Pale barracks near Ajdovščina 29 April 1952. (A. Smiljanić collection)

Yugoslav *Odred* in FTT and Forces of the Fifth Military District

Although it covered a different territory from 16 September 1947, the Yugoslav Army was the supreme authority in Zone B, and relations with the Allied military government in Zone A remained tense.[20] Subordinated to the military commander of the Yugoslav forces was the VUJA commander who acted as the local civil administrator. From 1947 to 1951 the VUJA commander was Colonel Mirko Lenac, and he was replaced in 1951 by Colonel Miloš Stamatović.

After the Free Territory of Trieste was formed, the Yugoslav *Odred* in the previous Zone A now became the backbone of the Yugoslav forces in the new Zone B. The other Yugoslav forces active in the various events of 1945-1947 now remained in the neighbouring garrisons in Yugoslavia. During the previous period the Yugoslav *Odred* formed part of the Allied contingent and had received its logistic support in the same manner as the American and British units. Now that it was in Zone B of the FTT its logistics and finance were a matter for the Yugoslav Ministry of Defence. In 1950 its Finance Department defined the means of finance of the Yugoslav Army *Odred* in Zone B, and its accounts and relations with the National Bank of Yugoslavia and Istrian Bank in Koper.[21]

The accommodation conditions for the Yugoslav *Odred* in Zone B were difficult and during the summer of 1951 eight barracks and four hangars were built to improve the living standards of the artillery regiment in Umag, since its personnel were living "in private houses and hotels". The *Odred* HQ in Portorož was also in poor condition too and its renovation started in July 1951.[22]

The 1st Proletarian Brigade remained as the core of the *odred* and it was stationed in Koper and surrounding villages. The Motomechanized Regiment most likely abandoned the Zone in autumn 1947, and was reorganized into VII Tank Brigade. In 1948 it was renamed as the 265th Motomechanised Regiment and stationed in the nearby town of Podgrad some 30 kilometres south-east from Trieste.

Under the organisation order issued on 24 July 1949 the Yugoslav *Odred* in Zone B FTT consisted of the following units:

- HQ with 584th AA Battalion in Portorož,
- 1st Rifle Proletarian Regiment in Koper, and
- 320th Artillery Regiment in Umag.

The 13th Proletarian Rifle Regiment, based in Tolmin and Bovec, seen on the march in 1952. (MCO)

In the "case of war" its HQ would move to the city of Pazin in central Istria, and the organisation would expand with the addition of the 145th Infantry Regiment, 762nd Communications Battalion, 803rd Pioneer Engineers Battalion and the 745th Medical Battalion, all of them mobilised in Pazin.[23]

The size of the *odred* could not be changed due to the treaty terms and the core units in Zone B remained the same. But in 1952, when Yugoslavia sided with NATO and started to receive US military assistance, the *odred* was reorganised and reequipped with new equipment which entered the Yugoslav inventory. In the "case of war" it would expand into the 46th Infantry Division. Besides the 1st Proletarian Infantry and 320th Artillery Regiment the *odred* controlled the 46th (ex-584th) AA Battalion in Portorož, the 46th Tank Battalion in Buje and 46th AT Battalion in Umag. It included also the 36th Infantry Regiment in Pula – which was outside the FTT – Zone B, and would join the *odred* in the case of war.[24]

One of the main expectations of the Yugoslav defence plan in the late 1940s, was that a future war would start exactly in the border region with Italy and the city of Trieste. The forces that were based in the nearby garrisons were under control of the Fifth Military District in Zagreb. The Fifth District maintained control over the previous Partisan IV Army which was renumbered in 1948 to the Tenth Army, and later in 1950 into the XXIII Corps. It had its HQ in Ljubljana and by the middle of 1948 it controlled 1st Proletarian, 22nd, 33rd, 54th, 56th and 60th Rifle Divisions. In the second half of 1948 the Tenth Army was downsized and the following rifle divisions were removed from its order of battle:

- 22nd Rifle Division (war-time Partisan 7th Banija Division) was disbanded in November 1948. At the beginning of the year it had its HQ in Idrija, and its three rifle brigades were in Ajdovščina, Tolmin and Bovec and its Artillery Brigade was at Crni Vrh.
- 54th Rifle Division (war-time Partisan 23rd Serbian Division) was transferred from Novo Mesto to Eastern Serbia, to strengthen the defence on the eastern borders of Yugoslavia.
- 56th Rifle Division (war-time Partisan 43rd Istrian Division) in Maribor, was subordinated to the HQ of the Twelfth Army in Zagreb.

In the area that surrounded the Free Territory of Trieste there remained three divisions and one mountain brigade. These were:

- 1st Proletarian Rifle Division, HQ in Postojna (1948) with three rifle brigades in Vipava, Sent Peter and Rakek and artillery brigade in Postojna. In 1949 it comprised of 65th Proletarian Rifle Regiment in Sent Peter, 124th Proletarian Rifle Regiment in Tolmin and Bovec, 106th Rifle Regiment in Ajdovščina and Vipava and 155th Artillery Regiment in Postojna.
- 33rd Rifle Division (war-time Partisan 17th East-Bosnian) Infantry Division, with HQ in Radovljica, three rifle brigades in Radovljica, Tržič and Kokra and artillery regiment in Kranj. In 1949 it comprised of 41st Proletarian Rifle Regiment in Metlika, 2nd Rifle Regiment in Celje, and 174th Rifle Regiment in Novo Mesto and 123rd Artillery Regiment in Črnomelj.
- 60th Rifle Division (war-time Partisan 26th Dalmatian) Infantry Division, with HQ in Ilirska Bistrica and three rifle brigades: in Ilirska Bistrica, Buzet and Podgrad and Artillery Brigade also in Ilirska Bistrica. In 1949 it comprised of 29th Proletarian Rifle Regiment in Ilirska Bistrica, 133th Rifle Regiment in Podgrad and Mučići, 10th Rifle Regiment in Klana and 30th Artillery Regiment in Ilirska Bistrica.
- 16th Mountain Rifle Brigade in Kranj with battalions in Radovljica and Tržič.[25]

The changes between 1948 and 1949 were caused by reductions in the number of troops and the renaming of brigades into rifle regiments, and later into infantry regiments.

The main strike force of the Fifth Military District was the 20th Tank Division:

- HQ in Kranj and which moved to Sisak in late 1948. It had the 265th Motomechanized Regiment in Podgrad, while two other tank brigades were in Vrhnika (268th – ex-1st) and Jastrebarsko (232nd – ex-2nd), all equipped with Soviet T-34 main battle tanks.

Artillery regiments which were under the direct command of the higher commands (Military District, Army/Corps) were located deeper in Slovenia:

- the 215th (122mm) in Velike Bloke and 202nd (122mm) in Ribnica.[26]

TRUST and BETFOR: Allied Forces in the FTT

The Allied Military Government continued to administer Zone A. They initially had at their disposal a 5,000-man strong force. Allied forces in the FTT consisted of the US contingent – Trieste United States Troops (TRUST) – and the British contingent – the British Element Trieste Force (BETFOR). The mission of TRUST and BETFOR was to maintain order in the Free Territory of Trieste and to support the policies of the Allied Military Government. Allied troops manned a series of 16 border outposts; TRUST soldiers manned Outposts 1 through 6; BETFOR troops manned Outposts 7 through 16.

TRUST was established on 1 May 1947 under Major General Bryant E. Moore, commander of the 88th Division. The core of TRUST was the 351st Infantry Regiment which remained from the 88th Infantry Division (the 88th Infantry Division, having completed its occupation mission in Italy, was inactivated 24 October 1947). On 23 February 1947 the regiment was ordered to move to Trieste to become part of the 5,000 troops representing the United States in FTT. "Since that time the Regiment has been occupied in the role of a garrison in Trieste. Training has been put to good advantage both in and out of garrison. There is an *Espirit de Corps* that cannot be beaten by any other unit in the United States Army."[27]

The HQ of TRUST was in Miramare castle, while the HQ of the 351st Regiment was in the village of Opicina, on a plateau just above the city of Trieste, with two of its infantry battalions stationed nearby and another infantry battalion stationed in Trieste. Non-regimental units were stationed at a number of locations in the free territory including the city of Trieste, the Opicina area and Duino.

The station list dated 13 June 1952 listed following US Army units belonging to TRUST force:

TRUST, HQ and HQ Company

351st Infantry Regiment (Headquarters and Headquarters company, three infantry battalions, each with a headquarters company, three rifle companies and one heavy weapons company, tank company (originally the separate 15th Tank Company), heavy mortar company and service company)

88th Armoured Reconnaissance Company,
281st Military Police Company,
23rd Ordnance Maintenance Company,
23rd Quartermaster Company,
9th Transportation Truck Company
17th CIC Detachment,
7th Sta Hospital,
537th Medical Svc Detachment,
98th Army Band,
7100th Allied Military Government Detachment,
7101st General Depot HQ and HQ Company
7102nd, 7103rd and 7104th AU Evacuee Detachments,
7105th Signal Svc Company,
7106th AU Engineer Svc Company and 7107th AU Engineer Gen. Svc Company and General Depot HQ and HQ Company.[28]

Page 20 THE BLUE DEVIL September, 1954

351st INFANTRY

The Spearhead Regiment

THE 351st Infantry, "Spearhead Regiment" of the 88th Infantry Division and veteran of victorious campaigns in France in World War I and Italy in World War II, is entering its eighth year as the line element of TRUST. Its mission in Trieste is best expressed by the following quotation: "It is a pledge of the United States of America to safeguard peace, to help reconstruct the economic stability of war-torn countries, and to establish the welfare of innocent peoples".

The Regiment was born in August 1917 as an Organised Reserve Regiment of the State of Minnesota, part of the 88th Infantry Division. For its part in the fighting in France during World War I the 351st Infantry had its colors decorated by General of the Armies John J. Pershing.

In 1919 the Regiment was demobilised in a ceremony at Camp Dodge, Iowa, site of its organisation. It was reconstituted in June 1921, still assigned to the 88th Division. The unit carried on in name only until the start of World War II, when it was returned to active duty on 15 July 1942. For the next seventeen months it trained intensively at Camp Gruber, Oklahoma, distinguishing itself in the Third Army's Louisiana Maneuvers by marching 62 miles in less than 48 hours. For this feat the Regiment was commended directly by Gen. George C. Marshall, then Chief of Staff, U. S. Army.

In November 1943 the 351st Infantry embarked for North Africa and landed there, part at Oran and the rest at Casablanca, in December. On 1 February 1944 the Regiment boarded the ships that were to take it to the scene of its biggest battles and its greatest achievements. Landing at Naples, it moved up to relieve elements of the 36th Infantry Division on the front.

Early in March the Regiment relieved a British unit near Minturno, and held the position throughout March and April; then, with the other elements of the 88th Division, it pushed on to Castelforte and to Santa Maria Infante, keystone of the formidable Gustav Line. Within 48 hours after the order to open fire had been given, a gap in the barrier had been breached and the road to Rome was open.

From the heights of Mt. Passasera, the Spearhead Regiment engaged in the offensive to gain Rome, and on the afternoon of 4 June broke into the Eternal City. Battles for Lake Albano, Tarquinia, Pomorance, Volterra and Laiatico followed, and for its part in the latter campaign the 3rd Battalion was awarded the Distinguished Unit Citation. In July the Regiment took part in the fight for the Arno River crossing, and from September to mid November the battle of the Gothic Line.

Long months on the Winter Line were followed by the storming of the Po River. After bitter fighting the 351st crossed the Po and pushed on to Verona, San Giovanni and Marostica. On the morning of 5 April 1945 the Regiment knifed into the Alps, and continued to drive the enemy north until the Nazi surrender on 2 May 1945.

At the completion of combat operations the Regiment had advanced from Naples to within 70 miles of the Brenner Pass, covering approximately 383 miles of some of the roughest terrain in Europe. During its 344 days of combat the unit had accounted for 40,000 enemy casualties and had destroyed large quantities of stores and equipment.

Eighteen members of the Regiment received Distinguished Service Crosses, and there were 650 lesser awards for valor. Over two-thirds of the Regiment won the Purple Heart. The Second Battalion won a Distinguished Unit Citation, shortly after the Third Battalion, for action in the battle for Mount Capello. Service and Medical Companies won the Meritorious Unit Citation, and the entire 88th Division was cited by the French Government with the Croix de Guerre with Palm.

In September 1945 the 351st Infantry took over the northern sector of the Morgan Line, with orders to maintain law and order along the Italian-Yugoslav border until the Peace Conference could establish a permanent boundary. On 23 February 1947 it was sent to Trieste (the Third Battalion had been in this area since July 1946) to form the main complement of the American garrison in the Free Territory of Trieste. On 15 November 1951 the 351st Infantry was allotted to the Regular Army.

Today the Regiment, although spread out through the Territory with casermas at Prosecco, Banne, and San Giovanni, carries on in its tradition as a top notch infantry outfit. Training hard and constantly, both in and out of garrison, and maintaining its well-known "esprit de corps", the 351st is still living up to its motto, "Toujours Pret"—Always Prepared.

TOUJOURS PRET

Caserma Prosecco, First Battalion.

Caserma Monte Cimone, Second Battalion.

Caserma Duca D'Aosta, Third Battalion.

Detail from *The Blue Devil* newspaper showing the history of the 351st Infantry Regiment. (BETFOR Association Official Website)

Another station list dated on 16 August 1954 showed some changes in the TRUST force order of battle:

7100th AU HQ, 7101st AU HQ Company, Special Troops
351st Infantry Regiment
88th Armoured Reconnaissance Company,
12th Field Artillery Battery (155mm howitzers, towed),
517th Engineer Company (Combat),
508th Signal Company,
281st Military Police Company,
17th Ordnance Battalion (Sep) – HQ and HQ Det,
23rd Ordnance Maintenance Company,
23rd Quartermaster Company,
17th CIC Detachment,
7th Sta Hospital,
537th Medical Svc Detachment,
98th Army Band,
7102nd, 7103rd and 7104th AU Evacuee Detachments and 7106th AU Engineer Maintenance Detachment.[29]

The most notable differences were the addition of a howitzer artillery battery, combat engineer and signal companies.

Table 3. TRUST commanding officers 1947 – 1954[30]

Major General Bryant E. Moore	May 1947 – June 1948
Major General William M. Hoge	June 1948 – March 1951
Major General Edmund Sebree	March 1951 – July 1952
Major General William B. Bradford	July 1952 – February 1953
Major General Bernice M. McFayden	February 1953 – July 1954
Major General John A. Dabney	July 1954– September 1954

The "British element of 5000 in the Free Territory of Trieste" was actually the 24th Independent Infantry Brigade – which remained after the withdrawal of the 56th Division in 1945/46. The British maintained the practice of rotating their battalions.

Table 4. BETFOR battalions from mid-1947

1st King's Own Regiment	May 1945 – May 1950
2nd Royal Scots Regiment	Jun 1947 – Dec 1948
2nd South Lancashire Regiment	Sep 1947 – Feb 1951
1st Cameronians Regiment	Dec 1948 – Dec 1949
1st Northhants Regiment	Nov 1949 – Sep -1952
1st South Lancashire Regiment	May 1950 – Feb 1951
1st North Staffordshire Regiment	Feb 1951 - Jun 1953
1st Loyal (North Lancashire) Regiment	Feb 1951 – Oct 1954
1st Suffolk Regiment	May 1953 - Aug 1954
2nd Lancashire Fusiliers Regiment	Jun 1953-Oct 1954

Besides the battalions there were units of Royal Artillery, Royal Signals, Royal Military Police (227 Provost Company), Royal Ordnance Corps, Royal Engineers, Royal Electrical and Mechanical Engineers (768 Static Workshop), Royal Army Medical Corps, Royal Army Service Corps, Intelligence Corps and Navy, Army, Air force Club.[31] The main of the British forces were based in the Rossetti Barracks in Trieste and Lazzaretto.[32]

For example, in the 1949, the Brigade was composed of the: 1st Battalion the King's Own (Royal Regiment) 2nd Battalion the South Lancashire Regiment (The Prince of Wales) and 1st Battalion the Cameroonians (Scottish Rifles).[33]

During 1948 the G (I) staff of the new HQ, now called BETFOR, amalgamated with the American intelligence staff to form G2 GSI. All of the British intelligence sections amalgamated to form a District Security Office which later became Trieste Security Office (TSO), about sixty strong. Although there was a joint headquarters, G2 GSI, the operational arms, TSO and the American CIC, remained separate. They did, however, cooperate and all reports were shared. In G2 GSI each office was staffed jointly by British and Americans and all papers were passed to both desks. TSO Office had comprised the largest field grouping of Intelligence Corps personnel ever assembled. There was also a detachment of MI6 in Trieste known as "The Chinese Laundry" to which TSO was sometimes asked to lend a hand. [34]

Two members of the Royal Military Police at the border outpost between Zone A and Yugoslavia in 1948. (John Pritchard/BETFOR Association Official Website)

Members of the Trieste Security Office, 21 July 1953. (BETFOR Association Official Website)

Italian Forces of the V Military Territorial Command in 1949

The Italian Army recovered after the Second World War and became a potential opponent to the Yugoslav forces in the case of eventual hostility. The allies provided important quantities of equipment for its rearmament, including such items as M4 Sherman tanks, M7 Priest self-propelled howitzers, and half-tracks.

Most of the forces that were deployed on its north-eastern borders were commanded by V Military Territorial Command with its HQ in Padova. It had two divisions and two brigades on strength:

Table 5. V Military Territorial Command in 1949

Unit	Composition
Motorised Infantry Division *Folgore* (HQ in Treviso)	182nd and 183rd Infantry Regiment, light armoured group 5th Lancieri, two artillery and one AA artillery regiment
Infantry Division *Mantova* (HQ in Gorizia)	59th, 76th and 114th Infantry Regiments, light armoured group 4th Lancieri, Naval Assault Battalion *San Marco*, three artillery and one AA artillery regiment
Armoured Brigade *Ariete* (with HQ in Pordenone)	132nd Armoured Regiment, 8th Bersaglieri Regiment, 132nd Self-propelled Artillery Regiment
Alpine Brigade *Julia* (HQ in Cividale del Friuli)	8th Alpine Regiment with two artillery groups and other miscellaneous units.

The V Command also had 5th Recruitment Centre, 41st AT Artillery Regiment and several of other minor units. It is important to note that the *Ariete* was the only one armoured brigade which Italian Army had at its disposal in 1949, and it was deployed in this part of the Italian territory.[35]

Communist Yugoslavia Becomes a US and NATO Ally

After the establishing of the FTT mutual incidents on its borders continued during the following period. In the first months of 1948 there were many incidents, such as patrols in vehicles or on foot crossing paths with one another, opening of fire (6 January, 22 March), violations of air space (at least 21 – mostly transport airplanes rarely reconnaissance missions) and violations of Yugoslav territorial waters. At the end of April 1948, the Allies limited traffic during night hours, which provoked further protests of the Yugoslav Military Authorities (VUJA).[36] During 1949, the stream of incidents continued, mostly referred to as the "provocations."[37] The most difficult incident occurred at the village of Dreka/Drenchia on the Italian side of Tolmin, on 26 April 1949, where one Italian solider was killed and two more were wounded.[38] More surprises were yet to come, however, as the "Iron Curtain" was about to move further to the east.

The turning point in Yugoslavia's policy after the Second World War occurred in 1948, when the Tito-Stalin dispute emerged into the open with the expulsion of the Communist Party of Yugoslavia from the Communist Information Bureau in June 1948.

Sir Robert Andrew of the TSO (later in charge of the Police Department at the Home Office) recalled the effects of Tito's breaking from the Cominform in 1948. When the news came through no-one knew what the implications would be and

> there was much speculation and excitement in TSO. Would the Red Army move into Jugoslavia to restore Moscow's authority? How would the local communist party in Trieste react? We were despatched in our jeeps to the border checkpoints, not knowing whether to expect to see Soviet tanks or a flow of refugees. In fact, at my particular checkpoint nothing appeared all day, except for an old woman in black with a donkey and some goats.[39]

After their first concerns diminished, the Allies started to realize that it could be useful to support Yugoslavia. On the other hand, after 1949 American (and British) officials could no longer define the Trieste problem even indirectly in terms of a Soviet-inspired threat and instead became primarily concerned with the local and Italo-Yugoslav implications of the dispute.[40]

The policy Planning Staff of the US State Department had been swift to explore the opportunities now opening up to sow maximum discord in this part of the Communist world. In 1950, US officials remarked that Yugoslavia was of direct importance to the security of the United States. As a result of this remark, it was decided that military and economic aid should be passed to Yugoslavia so that its potential for defence in facing the Soviet threat, could grow.[41]

The whole of 1951 saw negotiations between Yugoslav and US Army officials. The Yugoslavs strongly insisted on their priority needs, while the Americans insisted on improving Yugoslav capabilities to absorb new weapons and on American strategic intentions and priorities. Key meetings regarding the deliveries of the military aid took place during Colonel-General Koča Popović's (Yugoslav Chief of Staff) two visits to the United States. Even whilst negotiations were ongoing, deliveries of some weapons were made to the Yugoslavs, when some of the urgent

General Collins' visit was crucial for MDAP deliveries to Yugoslavia. Collins is seen here with Yugoslav Chief of the General Staff Koča Popović at Belgrade airport, in October 1951. (Archive of Belgrade via Aleksandar Životić)

Marshal Tito accompanied by General Koča Popović, and the Yugoslav state leadership, seen here during a discrete visit to Pula air base where he inspected the first deliveries of F-47D Thunderbolts. (*Muzej Jugoslavije*, Belgrade)

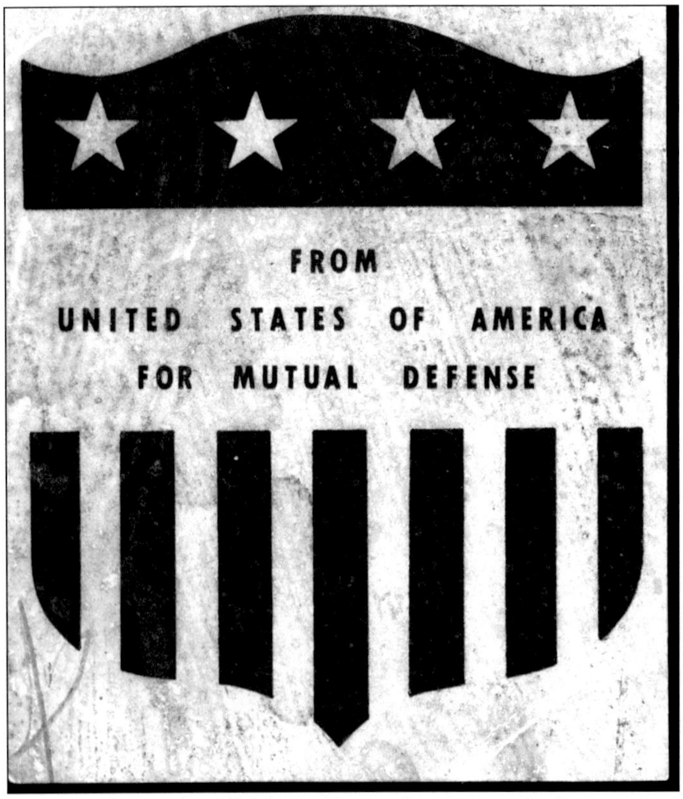

MDAP symbol used on all delivered items of equipment. (author collection)

needs were identified, including some artillery pieces, vehicles, and even some light aircraft.[42]

US officials explained that the war in Korea meant that there was a shortage of some armaments and equipment that the Yugoslavs needed. The Yugoslavs, for their part, tried to convince the Americans that they were interested only in up-to-date equipment, because they didn't plan to conduct partisan warfare in the case of Soviet aggression. Following the Second World War it was believed that the Yugoslav Army was a strong partisan type of army without a technical culture. Among the US Army officials there was an intention to pass to send military advisers to Yugoslavia together with the equipment.

Prior to signing of the Mutual Assistance Pact, several military exercises were performed for the Chief of Combined General-Staff General Collins, who visited Yugoslavia. The aim of his visit was to gather information about the Yugoslav Army's qualities and potential. The largest exercise took place in the Banja Luka area where armoured, airborne and aviation units were engaged in an assault over the Vrbas River. The Yugoslavs claim that this exercise impressed the US Army officials and led to the cancellation of the idea of sending advisers on a larger scale.[43]

The Military Assistance Pact (MAP) was finally signed between the officials of the Yugoslav and the US government in Belgrade on 14 November 1951. According to this pact, Yugoslavia was introduced into the framework of the Mutual Defence Aid Programme (MDAP) and Yugoslav orders for equipment could be fulfilled by the United States, Great Britain and France. The Yugoslav Parliament ratified the MAP on 9 January 1952 and described this act as resistance to the Soviet military threat and blockade, rooted in the principles of the UN.[44]

In an interview which coincided with the signing of the MAP, Marshal Tito stressed

> That military purchases from the United States do not mean change of our independent policy and specific development of socialism; we want that the United States supply us with particularities that we do not possess.

Tito added that strengthening of the Yugoslav military potential would contribute to the strengthening of stability and peace in southern Europe.[45]

Equipment deliveries within the framework of the MDAP enabled the *Jugoslovenska Narodna Armija* – JNA (*The Yugoslav People's Army*, the term "*People's*" was introduced on the 22 December 1951) a qualitative and quantitative growth through the 1950s.

The Yugoslav Air Force started to receive aircraft even before the MAP was signed. The first of these were 140 piston-engined de Havilland Mosquitos. These reached the Yugoslavian skies from late October 1951 onward.[46] By the beginning of 1952 deliveries of the Republic F-47D Thunderbolt fighter-bombers had begun. The Yugoslavs, who had an Air Force on the verge of collapse, welcomed these new "birds" with praise. Marshal Tito showed enormous interest in MDAP deliveries and was especially interested in the Air Force. In the middle of January 1952, he visited Pula air base to inspect the

Table 6. Major items of military equipment received by Fifth Military District between 1 November 1952 and 20 August 1953[50]

M4A3 Sherman tanks	281
M47 Patton tanks	97
M7 Self-Propelled Howitzer	22
M18 Self-Propelled Anti-Tank Gun	56
M36 Self-Propelled Anti-Tank Gun	9
M8 Armoured Car	63
M3A1 Reconnaissance Vehicle	27

newly delivered F-47Ds and expressed his great satisfaction in front of the airmen.[47]

A soldier of the 436th Border Brigade on watch on the mountainous border with Italy in 1950. (MCO)

Re-equipment of the Yugoslav Forces in "Ljubljana Gap"

The American and NATO intent was to strengthen the Yugoslav forces in the so-called Ljubljana Gap with the MDAP equipment, with the strategic aim of preventing the eventuality of a Soviet attack from the Hungarian plain towards northern Italy.[48] According to the plan the MDAP equipment was to be used to re-equip forces of the JNA Fifth Military District. The first unit which was fully re-equipped with the US equipment was the XXIII Corps with HQ in Ljubljana.[49]

Armoured vehicles supplied through the MDAP were passed to the units to replace mostly Soviet T-34 tanks and other vehicles. The quantities of armoured vehicles delivered enabled the 20th Tank Division to be fully re-equipped. In addition, each of the two Corps (XI and XXIII) would have their own tank brigades/regiments which was a step forward in the modernizing the units in the western parts of Yugoslavia. The next step was creating the tank battalions within each of the infantry divisions of the Fifth Military District formed in 1953 and later. Those were 1st and 6th Proletarian, 33rd, 56th and 60th Infantry Divisions as well as two divisions which would be formed in the "case of war" (46th and 137th), based in Postojna, Karlovac, Novo Mesto, Bjelovar, Maribor and Buje at FTT.[51]

Representatives of the NATO armies observing a Yugoslav Army exercise in 1952. (MCO)

In addition, the divisions of the Fifth Military District started to convert to the US equipment and vehicles. By the end of August 1953, 20th Armoured in Sisak and 60th Infantry in Ilirska Bistrica – closest to the FTT were fully re-equipped. Two other divisions in Maribor and Varaždin were rated as "mostly" converted, 1st and 6th Proletarian in Postojna and Karlovac and 33rd Infantry in Novo Mesto (which moved to Rijeka in 1953) were partly converted.[52]

The re-equipment of the Fifth Military District with MDAP equipment was carefully monitored by the members of the American Military Assistance Staff (AMAS). They were keen that Yugoslav military authorities do not pass the MDAP equipment to the units in the east of Yugoslavia, which was not of strategic importance to the Americans and NATO.[53]

Yugoslav tankmen examined M8 Greyhound armoured cars that had arrived in spring 1952. (MCO)

M47 Patton tanks with equipment, supplied through the MDAP, seen here while being unloaded in Rijeka harbour, mid-1953. (MCO)

Towards a New Division of the FTT

The changed Allied policy in the administration of Zone A was formally inaugurated in March 1951 when the new commander of the Allied forces, General John Winterton, arrived in Trieste. The previous policy run by General Airey was openly pro-Italian. On the contrary, Winterton took a much more neutral status and tried to establish better relations with the Yugoslav Military Government in Zone B. In April 1951, he was host to the new Yugoslav commander of Zone B, Colonel Milos Stamatović – an event which had never taken place during General Airey's administration.[54]

After the schism with Stalin, Tito's Yugoslavia started to pursue a kind of twofold policy towards the question of Trieste. While the Yugoslav government favoured partition, some of their lower level organisations on the ground still preferred to maintain a separate, independent, Free Territory.[55]

By the beginning of 1952, the Yugoslav position on the Trieste problem became much stronger than in the earlier period due to its much better relations with the Allies and NATO. But no matter the number of diplomatic initiatives, relations between Yugoslavia and Italy remained problematic. The Allies reached the conclusion that the only possible solution was the "freezing" of actual territorial status with some minimal corrections on both sides as the Allies considered that any kind of agreement between Yugoslavia and Italy was not possible. It was decided that the best solution was to formalize what was on the ground – zonal division of the Free Territory of Trieste.[56]

During the several meetings organized as part of the tripartite conference held in London on 9 May 1952 between the American, British and Italian representatives it was decided that most of the functions in Zone A should be passed to Italy. A memorandum kept the international presence though the existence of the Allied Military Commander who would maintain all the powers in Zone A. It was the first step in the annexation of Zone A to Italy.[57]

This division of zones A to Italy and B to Yugoslavia was discussed in the meeting between Tito and US ambassador Allen on 15 May 1952.[58] In public, Tito and Yugoslavia did not comment upon this division and mostly agreed with the proposal. In private however, Tito and the Yugoslav diplomatic circles were bitter and felt vulnerable. Tito expressed his negative attitude toward such a conclusion to the Trieste problem to Churchill on during his visit to London in March 1953.[59]

British Foreign Secretary Anthony Eden arrives in Belgrade 1952. His visit was a step forward in the solution of the Trieste problem. (MCO)

3
TRIESTE CRISIS 1953

Giuseppe Pella Government – Complicating of the Relations

A serious complicating of the relations between Yugoslavia and Italy began in mid-1953 when the less stable government of Alcide De Gasperi decided to take some radical measures connected with the question of Trieste.[1] This course was continued by the newly elected Prime Minister Giuseppe Pella who achieved power in August 1953. Yugoslav authors and some other historians have indicated that Pella decided to take these radical moves, since he was aware that Yugoslavia was about to start the next round of military negotiations in Washington to discuss ongoing strategic issues with the US, Britain and France. Much more, Yugoslav military officials used their unique strategic position at that moment to ask for more military assistance and mutual planning within NATO's framework against any possible Soviet aggression. As this news became clear in Rome, Pella decided to act, knowing that the outcome of the Washington negotiations could be an important trump card in the Yugoslav hand when the question of Trieste would be considered and took energic diplomatic steps to supress the negative effect of Yugoslavia getting closer to the West. Pella instructed Italian diplomatic and military representatives in all of the capitals of the Allied powers to express the dissatisfaction of the Italian government at the improvement of relations between NATO and Yugoslavia. Italian Chief of the Ground Forces General Staff, General Pizzorno, who was at that moment in the United States, warned his American colleagues not to rely on Yugoslavia too much. Pizzorno stressed that defence of the Mediterranean was "firmly closed and defended with the chain of the Atlantic [alliance] states: Italy, Greece and Turkey." The Italian ambassador in Washington, Tarchini made a protest to the State Department on the military negotiations between NATO and Yugoslavia, and the same protest was made to the Foreign Office in London. The argumentation of the Italian diplomats was that Italian public opinion and the government could not accept Yugoslavia's entry into, or any kind of connection with NATO.[2]

Yugoslav mountain troops of the 345th Brigade observing the border are with Italy, January 1952. (MCO)

Yugoslav-Italian border line. (MCO)

The newly elected Italian prime minister was not satisfied with the outcome of the Italian diplomatic initiatives against the connecting of Yugoslavia with NATO. Pella decided to take further action to force the Allies to cease performing a balancing act between Italy and Yugoslavia, and to strongly back Italy. He took the opportunity to react when the semi-official Yugoslav press agency *Jugopres* sharply attacked a speech in which Pella indicated "rethinking of the Yugoslav position" and mentioned "inevitable consequences."[3] The comment in *Jugopres* was seen by the Italian Government as proof that Yugoslavia was preparing to annex Zone B, and served as the pretext for Italy to

Members of the 436th Border Brigade observe the Italian side. Although armed with an MDAP-supplied M1 Thompson SMG, the soldiers have unusual peasant *opanci* foot-wear. (MCO)

activate its military forces. The British Foreign Office explained with delay, to the Yugoslav Government, that Italy made this move of its own accord and that NATO HQ was informed only much later. The Yugoslavs however, were convinced that neither the United States nor Great Britain had done anything to prevent the Italian course of action. Meanwhile, the Allies prepared a new step in resolving the Trieste Question and worked on a declaration which would mark the withdrawal of the Allied forces from Zone A and its handover to Italian governance.[4]

Incidents on the Mutual Border 1952-1953

In this period, the political and media tension between Yugoslavia and Italy was also manifest at their mutual border. The scale of incidents initially declined after Yugoslavia broke with the Soviets and their neighbours, however, the renewed political dispute over Trieste in 1952-1953 led to a rise of the number of the border incidents.

Compared with Yugoslavia's borders with Communist states where daily incidents ranged from incursions to killed border guards, on the border with the Italy there were no killed soldiers, infiltrated terrorist groups or other aggressive actions. There was no ideological dispute. Italian and Yugoslav temper give much flavour to those incidents that did occur however. Yugoslav military newspapers mainly portrayed those incidents as the outcome of the "immoral character of the Italian border guards". Italians were accused for petty theft, pornography and verbal and gesture provocations. But besides such provocations, there were nearly a dozen serious incidents in 1952 including following events:

- firing on Yugoslav soldiers (30 March at Mlinsko, 18-19 April at Nova Vas, 21 August at Neblo, 15 November in Gorizia and 2 December at Libek near Tolmin).
- violation of the Yugoslav air space (6 June at Vrtojba, 4 November at Prvačino).

The most unusual incident occurred on the 30 June, when a company belonging to the Italian 8th Alpine Regiment, some 65 soldiers led by their lieutenant, crossed the border. They climbed to the summit of Mangrt, a mountain of some 2,679 metres, at the most northern part of the Yugoslav-Italian border. The *Alpinis* took the opportunity to sign the guest book, cursing the Yugoslavs and writing provocative slogans.

Incidents with Italian fishermen in Yugoslav territorial waters were frequent in the whole period. The largest incident occurred on the night of 21-22 December 1952, when 24 fishing boats with over 170 men were caught by the Yugoslav Navy when they were fishing off the coast of Istria in the area between Pula and Rovinj. The Yugoslavs concluded that it was "characteristic that the incidents are connected to the diplomatic actions which immediately followed after." Similar incidents continued in 1953 and included firing with live ammunition or signal rockets on the Yugoslav side. Yugoslavia noted several "typically Italian provocations" including cursing Tito, incitement of the border guards to desert to Italy, offering cigars and other goods that were unavailable in Yugoslavia, and the appearance of prostitutes to tempt Yugoslav soldiers.[5]

In the summer of 1953, in the political atmosphere of the expected changes in the Italian Government, the incidents were on the rise. During August, there were many serious incidents: violations of Yugoslav air space (4, 17, 23 and 30 August), firing upon Yugoslav border guards (16 August), and the crossing of Yugoslav territory (23 at Hum, 30 at Bovec and 31 August at Gorizia).[6]

The first indication that Italian forces in the area were growing is dated 10 June 1953, when *Jugopres* reported that the

View across the disputed border: a Yugoslav solider and his Italian counterparts. (MCO)

Fifth Military District of the Yugoslav People's Army

Order of Battle Prior to the Trieste Crisis[10]

XXIII Corps HQ Ljubljana

1st Proletarian Infantry Division: HQ Postojna
- 3rd Proletarian Infantry Regiment – Sent Peter (Pivka)
- 13th Proletarian Infantry Regiment – Tolmin and Bovec
- 106th Infantry Regiment – Ajdovščina and Vipava
- 155th Artillery Regiment – Postojna
- Divisional units (communications, AD artillery, AT artillery, tank, self-propelled, engineer and medical battalions) – Postojna

33rd Infantry Division: HQ Novo Mesto
- 41st Proletarian Infantry Regiment – Metlika
- 59th Infantry Regiment – Celje
- 174th Infantry Regiment – Novo Mesto
- 123rd Artillery Regiment – Črnomelj
- Divisional units (communications, AD artillery, AT artillery, tank, self-propelled, engineer and medical battalions) – Novo Mesto

60th Infantry Division: HQ Maribor
- 11th Proletarian Infantry Regiment – Maribor
- 79th Infantry Regiment – Maribor
- 133rd Infantry Regiment – Ptuj and Murska Sobota
- 30th Artillery Regiment – Slovenska Bistrica
- Divisional units (communications, AD artillery, AT artillery, tank, self-propelled, engineer and medical battalions) – Maribor

Odred JNA – FTT: HQ Portoroz
- 1st Proletarian Infantry Regiment – Koper
- 36th Infantry Regiment – Pula
- 320th Artillery Regiment – Umag
- *Odred* units: 46th AD Artillery – Portoroz, 46th AT Artillery – Umag and 46th Tank Battalion – Buje)

345th Mountain Brigade – Kranj

XXIII Corps units:
- 268th Tank Regiment – Vrhnika,
- 202nd Howitzer Artillery Regiment – Ribnica,
- 423rd SP Artillery Regiment Ilirska Bistrica/Rakek,
- 435th Engineer Battalion – Celje,
- 308th Communications Battalion – Ljubljana,
- and other miscellaneous units and establishments.

XI Corps HQ Zagreb

6th Proletarian Infantry Division: HQ Karlovac
- 8th Proletarian Infantry Regiment – Delnice
- 9th Proletarian Infantry Regiment – Gospić
- 71st Mountain Regiment – Bihać
- 37th Artillery Regiment – Karlovac
- Divisional units (communications, AD artillery, AT artillery, tank, self-propelled, engineer and medical battalions) – Karlovac

14th Proletarian Infantry Division *Boris Kidric*: HQ Varaždin
- 10th Proletarian Infantry Regiment – Zagreb
- 14th Proletarian Infantry Regiment – Čakovec
- 178th Infantry Regiment – Murska Sobota and Ludberg
- 136th Artillery Regiment – Varaždin
- Divisional units (communications, AD artillery, AT artillery, tank, self-propelled, engineer and medical battalions) – Varaždin

56th Infantry Division: HQ Bjelovar
- 7th Proletarian Infantry Regiment – Virovitica
- 73rd Infantry Regiment – Koprivnica
- 140th Infantry Regiment – Bjelovar
- 55th Artillery Regiment – Bjelovar
- Divisional units (communications, AD artillery, AT artillery, tank, self-propelled, engineer and medical battalions) – Bjelovar

XI Corps units:,
- 411st AT Artillery Regiment Ilirska Bistrica/Rakek
- 127th Engineer Battalion Daruvar
- 326th Communications Battalion – Zagreb
- other miscellaneous units and establishments

20th Tank Division: HQ Sisak
- 232nd Tank Brigade – Jastrebarsko
- 265th Tank Brigade – Ilirska Bistrica and Podrgrad
- 372nd Self-propelled Regiment – Petrinja
- Divisional units (667th Communications Battalion, Overhauling Base No 5) – Sisak

Fifth Military District units:

- 202nd Howitzer Artillery Regiment – Ribnica,
- 215nd Howitzer Artillery Regiment – Velike Bloke
- 288th Artillery Regiment
- 159th AD Artillery Regiment – Zagreb
- 303rd AD Artillery Regiment – Zagreb
- 361st AD Artillery Regiment – Ljubljana
- 333rd Engineer Regiment
- 367th Communications Regiment Samobor
- 226th Artillery Observation Battalion
- 258th Pontoon Battalion
- 521st Chemical Battalion
- other miscellaneous units and establishments.

On the territory of the Fifth Military District were:
- 436th Border Brigade – Ljubljana
- 199th Border Brigade – Podravska Slatina
- Engineer School Centre– Karlovac
- Communications School Centre – Škofja Loka
- Artillery School Centres – Zagreb and Zadar
- Air Defence Artillery Centre – Zadar
- Military Technical Centre – Zagreb
- Reserve Infantry Officers School – Vipava
- Bases for acceptance of MDAP equipment: Petrinja, Zagreb-Prečko

Yugoslav patrol boat of the 31st People's Defence Naval Border Brigade stops an Italian fishing boat in the north Adriatic in 1953. The Yugoslav sailor is armed with an Italian Beretta sub-machinegun. (MCO)

Yugoslav Higgins torpedo-boats were also used in border control in 1953. (MCO)

Italian *Folgore* Division had been transferred to the border area to strengthen the *Mantova* Division already there. A group of Yugoslav Navy vessels sailed to Zone B on 21 June visiting the harbours of Koper, Izola and Piran, and the HQ of the Yugoslav Military Government in the FTT and its commander Colonel Milos Stamatović.[7] Ships of the Yugoslav Navy were also seen in Koper during July. Finally, the British news agencies reported that Italian armoured units had arrived in the vicinity of Gorizia on 31 August and that three warships had entered Venice harbour on 1 September.[8] Yugoslav press amplified its anti-Italian tune, and the Yugoslav government sent a handful of diplomatic notes to Italy.[9]

Pella's Plan to seize Zone A: Esigenza T

After the consultations with Minister of Defence Emilo Taviani and Chief of the General Staff General Efisio Marras, Italian Prime Minister Giuseppe Pella activated part of Italian ground forces and navy on the 29 August in response to an aggressive attack by the Yugoslav press agency *Jugopres*. The movement of the Italian vessels from Taranto harbour was confirmed by the Yugoslav naval attaché, who observed their movement along the south Adriatic coast. On the following day the Yugoslav official press agency *Tanjug* accused Italy of the creation of a "war psychosis", explaining that the movement of troops was not to take Zone A but to seize Zone B.[11]

Filippo Cappelano's recent research in the Italian archives provides us with details on this operation, named *Esigenza T (Trieste)*[Assignment "T"].[12] Following the orders of the prime minister, Italian Minister of Defence Paolo Emilio Tavani summoned Chief of the General Staff General Pizzorno on 28 August to discuss the alleged Yugoslav threat to occupy Zone B. He passed responsibility to Pizzorno to take pre-emptive military precautions in the matter. General Carlo Biglino, the commander of the V Army Corps in Padova was ordered to improve control of the situation on the eastern borders. The chief of the Operational Department of the General Staff was ordered to reconsider the possibility of a sudden occupation of Zone A.[13]

The Infantry Division *Trieste,* reinforced with the *Lancieri di Aosta* light armoured regiment, were ordered to prepare for this preventive action. The transport section of the General Staff was ordered to plan the movement of the division via railway from its base in the Emilia region to its point of debarkation in Friuli. The transport section advised that 54 trains and around 60 hours were needed for the transfer of the *Trieste* Division with all necessary equipment from Bologna railway station to the edge of Zone A. To preserve the secrecy of the operational planning and prevent the Yugoslav side from reacting, the Italian plan was to strengthen the V Corps without using troops which were assigned for NATO quick reaction.

The first Italian unit to be moved was the Light Armoured Regiment *Genova.* At the 06:30 a.m. on 29 August 1953, the regiment moved from Palmanova to Monfalcone and was placed under the responsibility of V Corps. On the the same day at 19:00 hours, the 76th Infantry Regiment was activated. It was reinforced with a battalion from 59th Infantry Regiment, two artillery batteries from 155th Artillery Regiment and a company from 114th Infantry Regiment. The reinforced 76th Regiment was deployed in the border area with Yugoslavia all the way from Tarbizio in the north to Monfalcone in the south. Soon after, two companies of the 183rd Infantry Regiment *Nembo* and Alpine Battalions *L'Aquilla* and *Tolmezzo* were added to this force. On the same day, the 51st Aerobrigata at Aviano was activated and moved up to a higher level of combat readiness.[14]

On the same evening of 29 August, representatives of the General

Staff of the three branches of the armed force gathered to prepare and send the operations directive for further action, code named *Delta*. The basic intention was to occupy Zone A in the FTT, with or without approval of the Allies. It predicted two phases: a rapid occupation of that territory with forces which were already stationed in the vicinity of the FTT and later consolidation of the positions with deployment of the *Trieste* Division.

The Delta Plan assumed that no force would be used against the Allied forces in the FTT, even if they were to take some pre-emptive actions. The Italian plan counted on surprise as an important factor, and it was supposed that Italian forces would infiltrate through the area of responsibility of the Allied force in the FTT and part of the force would be deployed through airborne and sea-landing operations. The Delta Plan assumed that no further actions would be taken against Yugoslav forces except in the case that they intervened in Zone A. In that case, they would just be ejected from Zone A, without expanding the combat operations into Yugoslav territory. Police forces in Zone A were to be in position to react and prevent any problems or unpredicted developments from occurring. At that moment, there was no information about the potential behaviour of the Allied forces in the Free Territory of Trieste.

The Italian General Staff approved this plan on the following day (30 August) and designated the units to carry out the operation. These were the *Genoa* Light Armoured Regiment, two battalions of the 8th Regiment of *Bersaglieri*, part of the *Novara* Light Armoured Regiment, two battalions of the marine infantry (*San Marco* and *Marghera*), a 300-man strong parachute unit, a company of the 5th Mortar Battalion, part of the 5th Communications Battalion and unit of *Carabinieri*. The General Staff ordered that all of its departments should organize the assembly of the certain specialists, such as drivers or tank crews, from other units, training centres and schools to fulfil the missing personnel in the units mobilised for this action.

Italian intelligence elements were also ordered to prepare for this action, and tasked to monitor the movements of the Yugoslav Army. They estimated Yugoslav forces in Zone B of the FTT as a single infantry regiment, two artillery regiments, an armoured battalion and marine infantry, engineer, communications and transport companies, totaling between 6,000 and 7,000 men.

The General Staffs of the Navy and Air force had also worked out the orders for their forces to take part in *Delta* on 31 August. Commanding officers for both navy and air force contingents were also designated as Admiral Giraldi Pecori and General Ranieri Cupini, respectively.

The naval forces tasked to participate in Operation *Delta* were organized into Naval Group Adriatic (*Gruppo Navale Adriatico*) commanded by Admiral Cappini, commander of the 2nd Naval Division. The group was subordinated to Admiral Pecori who established his HQ in Venice.

In addition to the above, these forces were supported by eight Lockheed P2V Harpoon patrol aircraft based at Verona-Villafranca and Grotagllie air bases, and 12 ASW and daytime reconnaissance S2C-5 Helldivers in Jesi and Grotagllie air bases. A total of 64 naval divers were in Spezia. Observation stations were set up at combat readiness, as were the defence forces in Taranto, Brindisi, Bari and Ancona harbour. There were also 200 mines ready in Brindisi harbour.[15]

Table 7. Naval Group Adriatic (Gruppo Navale Adriatico)

Duca degli Abruzzi and *Garibaldi*	Light cruisers
Artigliere, Aviere, Grecale, Altair, Alderban, Sirio, Clio, Aretusa and *Caliope*	Destroyers
12 *Gabbino*-class	Corvettes
Alabarda	Corvette
Alano, Mastino and *Bracco*	Auxiliary gunboats
Giada (from late October)	Submarine
811, 812, 821, 822, 832, 833 and *854*	Vosper torpedo boats
841, 843, 844 and *851*	Higgins torpedo boats
612 and *615*	CRD torpedo boats
Azalea, Biancospino, Mughetto, Primula, Gardenia, Dalia, Anemone and *Fiordalisio*	400-class minesweepers
303, 306, 310 and *313*	300-class minesweepers
VAS 712 and *722, DV 115* and *122*	Patrol boats
Proteo	Rescue ship
Stromboli	Transport ship
Sesia	Landing ship-water carrier
MTC 1101, 1102, 1104 and *1303*	Landing ships
20 MTP class and 15 MTM class	Landing boats

The Italian Air Force (AM), disposed three air brigades (*aerobrigate*) each of them equipped with three groups (equivalent to a USAF squadron) of Republic F-84G Thunderjets based at Verona-Villafranca (5 *Aerobrigata*), Ghedi-Montichiari (6 *Aerobrigata*) and Aviano (51 *Aerobrigata*). These three brigades had around 180 Thunderjets at their disposal and were subordinated to 56th Tactical Air Force with its HQ in Vicenza.[16] The AM General Staff added several other outfits for the "T" operations.[17]

The technological advantage of the Italian Air Force compared to the Yugoslav Air Force was formidable. At that time the Yugoslavs operated only 54 Thunderjets from Batajnica air base near Belgrade.[18] Comparing the naval potential, the Italian advantage was even more obvious: there were only 63,000 t. of the Yugoslav vessels comparing to an Italian 380,000 t. Moreover, the Italian Navy had developed a

Table 8: Italian Air Force Assigned Units for Operation "Esigenza T"

Parent unit	Unit	Air base	Type of aircraft
5th Air Brigade	101st Group	Verona- Villafranca	F-84G Thunderjet
	102nd Group	Verona- Villafranca	F-84G Thunderjet
	103rd Group	Verona- Villafranca	F-84G Thunderjet
6th Air Brigade	154th Group	Ghedi-Montichiari	F-84G Thunderjet
	155th Group	Ghedi-Montichiari	F-84G Thunderjet
	156th Group	Ghedi-Montichiari	F-84G Thunderjet
51st Air Brigade	20th Group	Aviano	F-84G Thunderjet
	21st Group	Aviano	F-84G Thunderjet
2nd Stormo	8th Group	Orio al Serio	F-51D Mustang
	13th Group	Orio al Serio	F-51D Mustang
4th Stromo	9th Group	Napoli-Capodichino	De Havilland Vampire
	10th Group	Napoli-Capodichino	De Havilland Vampire
46th Stromo	2nd and 98th Gruppo	Pisa	SM.82 and C.119

Torpedo-boats heading to the north Adriatic in September 1953. (MCO)

radar network which could monitor the movements of the Yugoslav Navy. On the contrary, the Yugoslav Navy did not have any kind of radar network on the shores, nor did it have devices to jam enemy radar surveillance.[19]

Commander of the V Corps, General Carlo Biglino, responsible for Operation Delta, asked for the political backing and support of the Allies for the occupation of Zone A. Biglino advised that he need 18 hours' notice to launch operation, which may have been possible by the 4 September. The General Staff reported that it did not expect that assistance from the Allies was possible at that moment.

On the following day, 2 September, General Biglino arrived in Rome to discuss the details of the operations. General Biglino expressed his concerns about the outcome of the operation in front of the Italian highest military circles. Surprise would be difficult to achieve and it would be very difficult to carry out the operation successfully with the forces assigned.[20] Biglino advocated a minor demonstration operation. The Italian Chief of the General Staff agreed with his commander in the field, and expressed his concerns asking what kind of political aims would be achieved.[21]

The movement of the Italian forces to the north-eastern borders was commented upon on 3 September by the Yugoslav Army magazine *Narodna armija*. Pointing to the movement of the Italian armoured units, *Narodna armija* sarcastically commented "God deliver us from such massive force!" The Yugoslav army magazine commented in similar fashion upon the Italian claims on the high level of the national spirit within the ranks of Italian Army "We know Italians. And they know us as well, to be misled with illusions that we, Yugoslavs, are scared of the movements of their Navy, 'armoured divisions', 'tanks and military vehicles.' *Narodna armija* concluded the "Italian blackmail campaign – scares nobody, frightens nobody."[22]

Tito's Speeches Add More Fuel to the Emerging Conflict

September did not bring a decline of tensions. The Yugoslav press continued to count the Italian military movements and reports, although inaccurate, from the border area claimed that in the area between Gorizia and Zone A several Italian divisions were deployed, naming *Mantova* – around Gorizia, *Centauro* between Gorizia and Doberdob and *Ariete* at the border of the FTT. The Yugoslav newspaper *Borba* almost daily counted the numbers of the Italian military vessels which were seen in the harbour of Venice. That number reached 12 warships, with the cruiser *Duca degli Abruzzi* among them carrying Admiral Lucano Biggi aboard. Italian officials rejected the accusations on alleged provocations, as well as the official Yugoslav note on this matter.[23]

Neither Tito's nor Pella's addresses to massive gatherings and public meetings indicated the easing of tensions. In the large meeting held on 6th September to celebrate 10 years of the liberation of the Slovene Littoral from Italian rule, Tito made an important speech. The meeting was held in the vicinity of the Italian borders, in the hamlet of Okroglica, some 20 kilometres east from Nova Gorizia. Here Tito announced the abandoning of the compromise solution to the Trieste question. Previously, in talks with Western diplomats he agreed to the zonal division with some corrections. Now he radicalised his standpoint saying "We are interested in the whole Free Territory of Trieste. Not just Zone B, but Zone A too. Our people live there too…" He described the division of the FTT as the "unhappy thing", since it did not care about the interests of the people who lived there. The Yugoslav leader made his new request "Trieste should be [an] international city while the entire Slovenian inland should be annexed to Yugoslavia."[24]

Tito sharply warned Italy "it cannot be characterised different that as the act of the aggression… no matter that there were no clashes so far". He added "we still have the time to send the divisions and supress the enemy to take out his intentions."[25] *Narodna armija* which reported from this huge gathering, called the Italian military action the "unsuccessful military-diplomatic comedy of Rome" and "Don Kihot's [Quixote's] move of the Giuseppe Pella" adding a handful of accusations on Italian fascism, terror against the Slovenes and cowardice of the Italians in the Second World War: "We have seen their divisions. Not just one or two... armed and disarmed."[26]

Tito's request that the whole FTT should be annexed to Yugoslavia, and Trieste should be an international city, provoked a series of negative reactions on the West. It was perceived as Yugoslav blackmail, mostly influenced with the signs of normalisation of its relations with the Soviet Union after Stalin's death in March 1953.

At the following meeting in Split on 13 September, Tito replied to the negative reactions of the West to his new standpoints on the Trieste question. Tito expresses surprise at such reaction adding that this suggestion is "realistic and imbued with our victims…" the Yugoslav leader pleaded "we do not ask for the people abroad to be

Table 9: Eskadra of the Yugoslav Navy Warships Deployed at the Beginning of the Crisis[28]

Unit	Harbour of Deployment	Warships on Strength
Eskadra HQ	Piran, Zone B (home base: Šibenik to Pula)	*Istranka, Mornar*
6th Destroyer Squadron	Koper, later moved to Piran, Zone B (home base: Šibenik)	51 – *Triglav*, 52 – *Biokovo*, 53 – *Durmitor*, 54 – *Učka*
11th Torpedo-boat Squadron	Umag and Novigrad, Zone B (home base: Šibenik to Rijeka)	TČ-106 TČ-108, 109, 110, 111, 112, 113, 114, 115, 116 117,118, 132, 133, 150, 151, 152, 153 and 159 TČ-301, TČ-391 and 392
38th Patrol-boat Squadron	Koper and Izola, Zone B (home base Kardeljevo-Ploče to Rijeka)	PBR 501, 502, 503, 504, 505, 506, 507 and 508
76th Torpedo-boat Squadron	Poreč (home base: Kumbor)	TČ-120, 124, 125, 127, 128, 129, 131, 136, 137, 139, 141, 142. 143, 146 and 147
25th Guards Naval Detachment	Pula – Brioni Islands	TČ-127, 128, 129 and 130
22nd Auxiliary Ships Detachment	(Home base Split)	24 different auxiliary ships

Yugoslav destroyers 51 *Triglav* and 52 *Biokovo* of the 6th Destroyer Squadron. (MCO)

on our side, but just to be objective" and "not to produce some kind of one-sided conclusions and agreements without our knowledge and against our will."[27]

Yugoslav Army and Navy Activities

The Yugoslav military leadership did not react immediately to the Italian movements. On 5 September it ordered that the *Eskadra* of the Yugoslav Navy should create a Mixed Joint Force (*Mešoviti združeni odred* – MZO).

The MZO Force would have nearly all of the combat vessels on the fleet list of the Yugoslav Navy and was tasked, together with the 1st Proletarian Infantry Division with its HQ in Postojna, the JNA Detachment in Zone B, and air force, to "prevent entry of the foreign troops in Zone B and its further advance towards Istria, prevent the intrusions in territorial waters of Zone B and Istria and forcibly act against the violations of air space made by the Italian Air Force over Zone B and Yugoslavia".[29]

It took a whole week for the Yugoslav Navy to prepare the vessels for the MZO force and full combat readiness was reached on 12 September. On that day, two of the Yugoslav destroyers sailed from Šibenik to Rijeka, and two days later on to Pula, which was the concentration point for all of the MZO/*Eskadra* warships. The *Eskadra* HQ was already in the city, deployed aboard the auxiliary ships *Istranka* and *Mornar*. Its commander, Admiral Josip Černi (who in 1945 had been the first Yugoslav commander of Trieste) received orders upon which he issued further organisational orders and combat guidelines for carrying out the task and movement of his warships into Zone B.[30] Those combat guidelines defined the level of combat readiness, procedures and other necessary steps for various situations that may have occurred when the warships reached Zone B. It was estimated that the training of the crews was at a satisfactory level and annual combat training and live firing had already finished. Basic tactical actions and joint sailing in formation were already trained for but the crews and units of the MZO were not trained in the joint combat operations and cooperation with the air force.[31]

On 3 Spetember, Italian intelligence reported on the Yugoslav troop movements from Maribor, Ljubljana and Zagreb scheduled for 9 September. They reported intensive activities by the Yugoslav border guards, as well as the arrival of the armoured columns in the area of Solkan in border area of Gorizia. On the other side, it seems that the estimation of the Italian General Staff led to a decline of the tension within their forces: on the 5 September, leave into the city was allowed for soldiers of the units which were deployed on the border, and from 9 September the forces on the border were reduced.

On 10 September, the Italian Chief of the General Staff started studying of the occupation of Zone A, counting on agreement with the Allies and the replacement of Allied troops with Italian forces. From 14 September, the Italian General Staff ordered a significant downscaling of the deployment of its forces towards the border of Italy and Zone A. The Alpine Brigade was ordered to return to its garrison and five days later, Chief of the General Staff ordered another group of the deployed forces to return to bases and leave the border line to a couple of companies of the *Genoa* Armoured Cavalry Regiment. After 21 September the forces which were tasked for operations *Delta* and *T* were ordered to send five percent of their personnel on leave.

Meanwhile, the Italian General Staff finished a new version of the *Delta* plan on 15 September. It again planned the advance of Italian troops into Zone A using all existing roads and communications, reaching the borders of Zone B and Yugoslavia. Now, the emphasis of the Italian General Staff was in the speed of the reaction rather than its constituents. By increasing the speed, it was planned that the forces which entered Zone A would reach as far as they could, thus minimizing the eventual Yugoslav reaction.

The ground contingent relied on the *Trieste* Infantry Division. It was reinforced with self-propelled artillery and parts of the *Cremona* Division, which was also tasked to take action along with the bulk of the reinforced *Trieste* Division. The naval echelon consisted of three battalions, among them one of the *Bersaglieri*. The airborne operation was limited by the transport capabilities of the Italian Air Force to land forces only up to the level of a paratrooper battalion.[32]

In mid-September, the Yugoslav side continued to inform the public of the growth in the Italian troops in the area ofTrieste, focusing on their weak morale. On the 12 September the *Borba* daily brought the estimation that 35,000 Italian troops were deployed on the borders with Yugoslavia and gave the details of the Italian Army order of battle. The Yugoslavs estimated that the number of the available aircraft at Pordenone, Aviano and Udine air bases was around 90. As usual, the Yugoslav press continued to inform of the tactical movements alongside the border, violations of the border and especially of Yugoslav airspace which had arisen in September. The news included reports of troop movements, and the captures of Italian fishermen with their ships in Yugoslav territorial waters.

Such incidents continued until 8 October, the first day of the outbreak of the crisis. *Borba* reported the case of a defected Italian conscript named Remo Mikelica. He was a solider in the 78th Infantry Regiment and deserted to Yugoslavia on 16 September. Mikelica reported on the deployment of his regiment since activation and alleged low morale among the Italian troops – "Panic and war psychosis reached the culmination in the 78th Regiment few days prior the celebration in Okruglica… Most of the soldiers were in a fear of war, and many of them cried." On the same day it was reported that an Italian officer named Mario Cordinalni deserted to the Yugoslav side with a lorry and weapons. But there were no further details on this deserter[33]

There were also Yugoslav desertions in the same period. Yugoslav pilot Lieutenant Nikola Jakšić from the 111th Fighter-Bomber

Two destroyers 53 *Durmitor* and 54 *Učka* heading to the north Adriatic. (MCO)

The 2nd Tank Brigade was established in the Soviet Union in March 1945, deployed to Yugoslavia and then took part in combat operations starting in mid-April 1945. All of its vehicles were painted in olive drab overall: in addition to its turret number, this tank also received the inscription *Živio Maršal Tito* (Long Live Marshal Tito) on its gun barrel and *Oslobodioci* (the Liberators) on the tool box. The Yugoslav tricolor with the Red Star (which subsequently became the official flag of Yugoslavia), was frequently added on a pole attached to the rear of the turret for easier identification. (Artwork by David Bocquelet)

Starting in 1952, the JNA received a large number of M3A1 White Scout Cars under the Mutual Defense Assistance Program (MDAP). As far as is known, all were left in standard olive drab colour, and usually retained their US maintenance stencils in white. The JNA added the vehicle's registration – 4464 in this case. This M3A1 served as a command vehicle of an unknown self-propelled artillery battalion deployed in the Kras area as of October 1953. (Artwork by David Bocquelet

Another type provided through the MDAP in 1952 was the M8 Greyhound armoured reconnaissance car. As usual, these were left in olive drab overall, and retained their US stenciling, while receiving the JNA registration 4225 on the turret. As of September 1953, this vehicle was operated by the 232nd Tank Brigade of the 20th Armoured Division and deployed in the Jastrebarsko area. (Artwork by David Bocquelet)

The JNA had operated a small number of US-made vehicles since the 1944-1945-period but received even more of these through the MDAP in 1952. This M4A3/76 Sherman was left in olive drab overall, to which the white JNA registration 3246 had been added by the time it was deployed to the Trieste area by the 20th Armoured Division (V Military District), in September 1953. More than obvious is the big inscription on the side of the hull, reading *mi smo Titovi – Tito je naš* (We are Tito's – Tito is Ours!) – which was one of the characteristic inscriptions, usually applied with chalk, during the field exercises held in September 1953. (Artwork by David Bocquelet)

Also provided under the MDAP in 1952 was this M7B2 Priest 105mm Gun Motor Carriage. Painted in olive drab overall, it received the JNA registration 4679 and was assigned to an unknown self-propelled artillery regiment of the 20th Armoured Division as of October 1953. (Artwork by David Bocquelet)

The most powerful addition acquired by the JNA thanks to the MDAP became the M47 Patton main battle tanks. As usual, all were painted in olive drab overall: the sole Yugoslav addition consisted of the – unusually large – registration number 3707. The vehicle, seen with turret traversed for transit, was assigned to the 268th Brigade: originally the 1st Yugoslav Tank Brigade, established in Italy in July 1944 as a part of British support for Tito's Partisans, this was the first unit to receive M47s, only about half a year before the outbreak of the crisis of 1953. (Artwork by David Bocquelet)

Bersaglieri, 8th Reggimento Bersaglieri, Italian Army
The 8th Bersaglieri Regiment of the new Italian Army of the post-war period, wore a green woolen uniform introduced in the early 1950s, which showed strong US influence – both in its design as well as in colours. The example seen here has the *cordoni verdi* (green cords), tied to the body, characteristic of this centuries-old Italian formation. Inset is shown the *il fregio* – the traditional symbol of the Bersaglieri. (Artwork by Anderson Subtil)

Sergeant, Military Police, 88th Infantry Division, Trieste United States Troops (TRUST), US Army
US occupation forces in post-war Europe generally performed their service wearing the well-known 'Ike' jacket and colorful M1 helmets, often wearing just the inner plastic helmet-liner. In the case of this sergeant, the badge between the letters MP on the helmet is the one of TRUST ("Trieste US Troops"), shown in detail above the left shoulder of the figure, and based on the insignia of the US 88th Division. The leather belt is in the Sam Browne style and the holster is of the model M1916, created specifically for the Colt M1911 pistol. (Artwork by Anderson Subtil)

One of the M36B1 Jackson Gun Motor Carriages – essentially the M36 on the chassis of the M4A3 Sherman tank – assigned to the V Corps of the Italian Army as of mid-1953, and as preserved in the Museum of the *Ariete* Armoured Brigade in Pordenone. The Italian army used to apply the national tricolore and tactical signs (including the vehicle's registration, 5941 in this case) on the front and the rear hull, and the divisional or brigade insignia on the turret side. In addition to the armoured divisions, M36s were also assigned to independent artillery regiments. (Artwork by David Bocquelet)

Lance Corporal, Military Police, British Element Trieste Force (BETFOR)
The Battle Dress used by this MP belonged to the model introduced by the British Army in 1949, and was slightly different to the version used during the Second World War. That said, this uniform was the only conventional element of his clothing: the rest was specific to British Military Police officers, and included the typical Redcap and the 1937 white webbing for pistol (containing the classic Webley Mk IV caliber .38 revolver). Inset is shown the emblem of the 24th Infantry Brigade (used as the symbol of the entire BETFOR). (Artwork by Anderson Subtil)

Machine gunner 1st Proletarian Rifle Division, JNA
Although closely resembling that of the German Wehrmacht of the Second World War, the uniform of this Yugoslav soldier deployed in the Trieste area of late 1940s is actually of Yugoslav design and origin. On the contrary, the Model 1942 steel helmet and the belt came from stocks captured during the Second World War. The braces re made of leather and the short boots were manufactured locally. An additional item, not shown here, would be the 'Titovka' cap, worn by all JNA troops, regardless their rank and period: troops deployed in the Trieste area during second half of 1945 were usually issued with caps in dark blue, rather than the regular grey-green. This soldier's armament is the legendary German-made MG42 (7.92x57mm caliber). Notable is the carrying case attached to the belt, containing weapon-cleaning utensils. (Artwork by Anderson Subtil)

Willys Jeep, serial M5236543, BETFOR Military Police, British Element Trieste Force (BETFOR), Trieste, early 1950s
Like nearly all American, British and Italian military vehicles of the early 1950s, the ubiquitous Willys Jeeps of the British Element Trieste Force were pained in olive drab overall. They wore the inscription 'Military Police' on their windshields, and often the insignia of their parent formation (this Jeep was drawn from the 24th Infantry Brigade, the symbol of which was used by the entire BETFOR). (Artwork by David Bocquelet)

Republic F-47D Thunderbolt serial number 13032/032 (ex-USAF 45-49202A) of the 111th Fighter-Bomber Regiment, 37th Aviation Division, JRV, Cerklje AB, autumn 1953. Delivered through the MDAP in early 1952, this Thunderbolt was left in its original 'bare metal overall' livery, with a matt-black anti-glare panel along the upper fuselage. The JRV roundel was applied in the place of former USAF markings and was only few centimeters narrower. (Artwork by Tom Cooper)

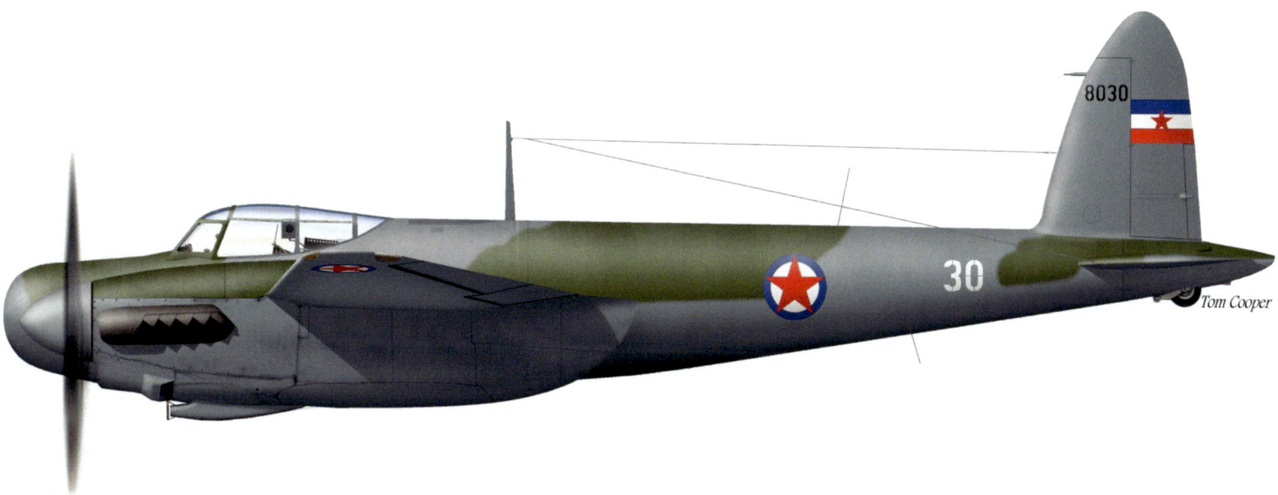

De Havilland Mosquito NF.Mk 38 serial number 8030/30 (ex-RAF VT-696) of the 103rd Reconnaissance Regiment, Pleso Air Base (AB), autumn 1953. Like the majority of the JRV's Mosquitoes, this aircraft – delivered to the JRV in late November 1951 – was left in the dark green and PRU blue camouflage applied prior to delivery. This was sometimes, though not always, badly worn out by the weather and intensive use. The fuselage roundel was the RAF standard, and had merely the Red Star applied atop of it. (Artwork by Tom Cooper

This De Havilland Mosquito FB.Mk VI serial number 8064/64 was assigned to the Aviation Test Centre, at Zemun Air Base, as of 1952-1953. While painted in standard RAF camouflage pattern consisting of dark green and PRU blue, it also received the Red Star applied directly atop the RAF roundel on the fuselage. The aircraft was initially used for various trials before being assigned to the 32nd Bomber Division based at Pleso AB, outside Zagreb: by the time of its retirement in 1963, it was one of the last Mosquitoes flown by the JRV. (Artwork by Tom Cooper)

This Ikarus S-49C wore the serial number 2405 and was assigned to the 185th Aviation Regiment, an element of the Air Officers School based at Ljubljana Polje airfield, as of October 1953. It was delivered to this unit straight from the Ikarus factory in September 1953, painted in 'pigeon grey' or medium sea grey (BS381C/637) overall, and received standard JRV insignia: its fin- and wing-tips were painted in white while the 185th Aviation Regiment was acting as 'aggressor', during the field exercises of September 1953. (Artwork by Tom Cooper)

In 1947, Yugoslavia received a large number of Messerschmitt Bf.109s and Ilyushin Il-2 Shturmoviks from Bulgaria. All the Il-2s in question received what became the essence of the future standardized JRV camouflage pattern consisting of medium sea grey (BS381C/637) on top surfaces and light blue on undersurfaces. As of October 1953, this example – serial number 4156/56 (construction number 308466, manufactured in 1945) – was assigned to the Cerklje-based 37th Aviation Division. It remained in service until 1955. (Artwork by Tom Cooper)

A reconstruction of the Republic F-84 Thunderjet serial number 10547/47 (ex-USAF 52-8381) assigned to the 117th Fighter Regiment, 44th Aviation Division JRV, Batajnica AB, as of first week of October 1953. As usual for ex-USAF aircraft of this period, it was left in its 'bare metal' overall finish, with the upper side of the fuselage painted in olive drab. Unless removed, all the USAF maintenance stencils were left in their place. The Yugoslav national insignia was applied instead of earlier USAF insignia, and the national flag over the USAF serial on the fin. This aircraft remained at Batajnica during the Trieste Crisis, but was subsequently passed to the 204th Regiment (at the same base). (Artwork by Tom Cooper)

A North American F-51D Mustang, serial 2-24 of the 2° Stormo, Aeronautica Militare (Italian Air Force), Vincenza, 1950-1953. Like Yugoslavia, so also the Italian air force of the post-Second World War period was rebuilt through acquiring a mix of indigenous designs, and a few British and US-made aircraft provided through the MDAP. This Mustang was left in its bare metal overall finish, with a black anti-dazzle panel in front of the cockpit. National insignia was applied in six positions and serials – in very stylish digits – on the rear fuselage. Inset is shown the insignia of the 2° Stormo. (Artwork by Tom Cooper)

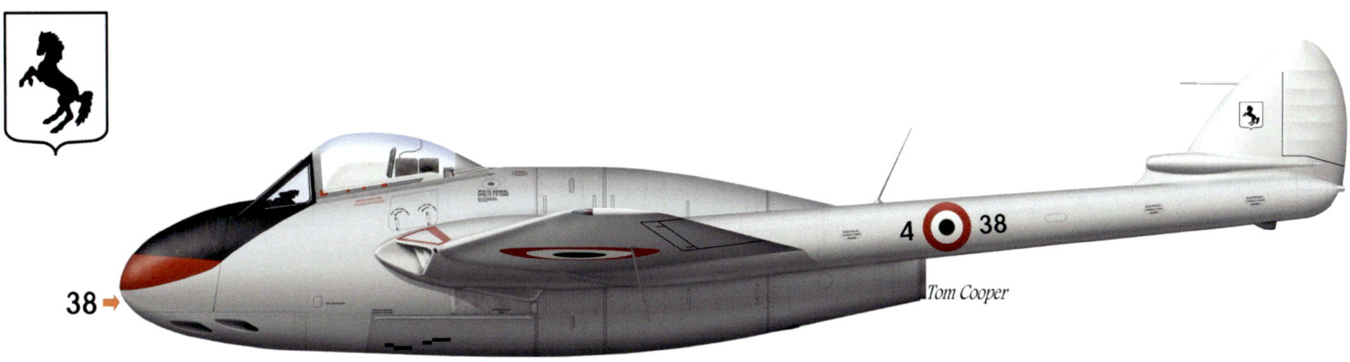

A de Havilland Vampire FB.Mk 52 serial 4-38, of the 4° Stormo, Napoli/Capodichino AB, 1953. Left in its high-speed silver finish overall, this Vampire received the 'anti glare panel' in black and in form typical for examples manufactured by the Italian company Aermacchi of the early 1950s. This was 'underlined' through the addition of a red colour, creating a kind of 'mouth' impression. National insignia was applied in six positions (notable are unusually large roundels on undersurfaces of the wing) and the unit insignia – the famous black prancing horse – on a small white shield, outlined in black, on the fin. (Artwork by Tom Cooper)

Exactly like the JRV, so also the Italian Air Force received Republic F-84G Thunderjets from the USAF. This example, serial number 51-6 (ex-USAF 51-10780) was assigned to the 20° Group of the 51° Stormo, based at Aviation AB in September 1953. Its bare metal overall finish was 'enhanced' through extensive application of a bright red colour to the nose, wing-tip drop tanks, the rear fuselage and the fin. The 'box' on the fin came from an unpainted area containing the original USAF serial, which was retained: the title U.S.A.F. was removed though. National insignia was applied in six positions. (Artwork by Tom Cooper)

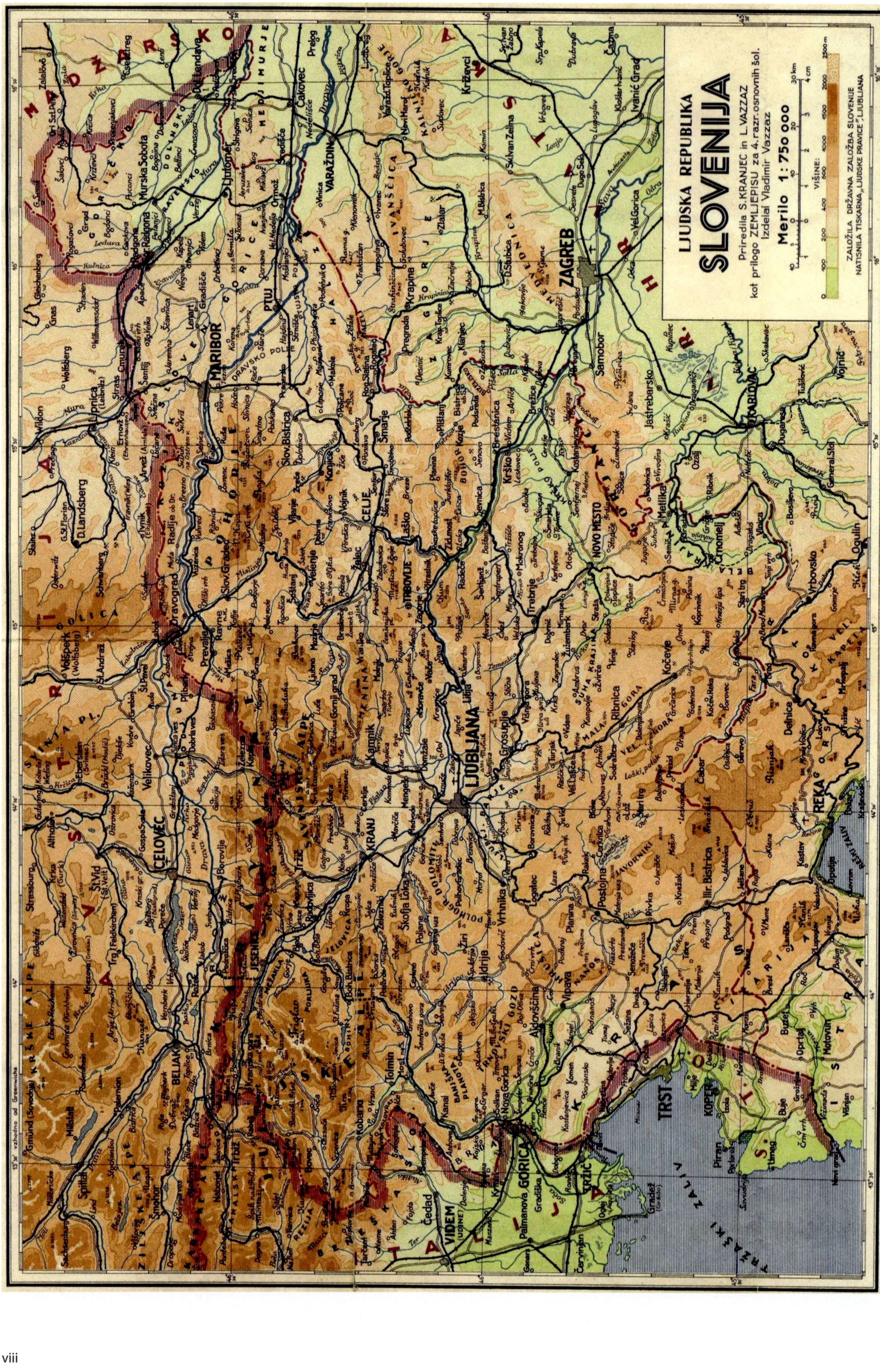

Official map of the People's Republic of Slovenia (itself then a part of the Federal People's Republic of Yugoslavia) and the Free Territory of Trieste (marked with abbreviation S. T. O.), from 1952. (Bojan Dimitrijevic Collection)

Thunderbolts of the 111th Regiment, under camouflage netting, during manoeuvres in September 1953. (M. Micevski collection)

The preparation of M4A3/76mm Sherman tanks of the 232nd Tank Brigade, September 1953. (MCO)

Aviation Regiment defected from Cerklje air base with an F-47D Thunderbolt and landed to Aviano. Jakšić explained to the Italians that he had been planning to leave Yugoslavia for a long time, since Partisans killed his mother during the war. He took advantage while his fellow colleagues were listening Tito's speech in Spilt on radio that day, took the plane and left for Italy. After landing, Jakšić climbed out of the cockpit, ripped the red star from his cap and reported to the local AM commander, asking for asylum. What was a considerable surprise for the Italians was that a Yugoslav Thunderbolt reached Aviano unnoticed by any of the Italian forces, from crossing the border to landing.[34]

Another interesting comment reported by *Borba* in this period was that the Italian military attaché in Belgrade, Colonel Tomaso Caliseo, was allegedly questioned in Italy "since his positive statement on the power and readiness of the JNA." Caliseo allegedly made such a statement after the large Yugoslav manoeuvres was "learned [of] in the Italian Ministry of Defence."[35]

Massive JNA Exercises in Croatian Zagorje

During the rise in Italo-Yugoslav tensions, Tito's army was occupied with the preparation and carrying out of large manoeuvres in the Zagorje area, north of Zagreb (Croatia). The Yugoslav Army actually had prepared and organized this large-scale manoeuvre not as a show force to the Italians but to show the NATO allies the level of the Yugoslav adoption of the MDAP equipment and to demonstrate the defence of the Ljubljana Gap, a pass between the Hungary and Italy, which was regarded as one crucial for the defence of the whole of Western Europe.

On 14 August 1953, Marshal Tito signed the order for manoeuvres scheduled for September. The Fifth Military District was responsible and its commander General Kosta Nadj would be the commander of the exercise. Tito's order also regulated the mobilisation of the reservists to fill the units engaged in the exercises up to the necessary scale. The first exercises at regimental level started in the second-half of August.[36] Most of the troops of the Fifth Military District which took part in the manoeuvres were actually moved into the area where exercises would be undertaken: north-east from Zagreb. On the Italian "front" 1st Proletarian Division remained, as did the detachment in

Zone B and the already engaged naval forces.[37] The call issued for the mobilisation of the troops was followed by rumours, among them that the mobilisation was actually intended for the "war with Italians."[38] The total of engaged active and reserve forces reached the number of 50,000 troops.[39]

The manoeuvres started on 14 September with the 20 kilometre-dash towards Zagreb of the "Blue" force (aggressors) in this case acting as Hungarian or Soviet forces. The advance of the aggressors lasted for six days, consolidation took two days and on 23 September the retreating Yugoslav forces launched a successful counter-attack, surrounded, and then destroyed the enemy.[40] It is interesting that even with the growth of the crisis with Italy, the Yugoslav General Staff planned the manoeuvres with a scenario where they had to count on Allied and Italian help in providing logistics and other assistance. In reality a Soviet/Hungarian strike over the plains would be difficult to stop without the flow of assistance from the Adriatic and over the Italian border into the Ljubljana Gap, including assistance from the Allied forces in the FTT and Italian army as well. The Yugoslavs avoided such scenario intentionally with the intention of showing NATO Allies their importance in defence of the Ljubljana "Gap".

Marshal Tito visited the manoeuvres with a variety of Yugoslav and foreign guests, including British Field-Marshalls Montgomery and Harding who were the most notable Allied guests. In addition there was also Chief of the American Assistance Staff General Harmony with his men, the Deputy Chief of the General Staff of the Greek Army and high-ranking delegations from the US, British, French and Turkish armies.[41] Field Marshal Montgomery who was at the moment Deputy SACEUR, received extraordinary attention and his visit covered the whole of the exercise. He met different Yugoslav military and political representatives, while he spent only a couple of hours at the manoeuvre itself visiting just a single regimental HQ. Monty expressed satisfaction with what he had seen, praising the Yugoslav Army – "It is [an] excellent Army". Montgomery spent most of his visit touring the Adriatic coast. Yugoslav military officials noted that Deputy SACEUR explained that they should not take the Italian threats "seriously" and that their forces were under the NATO command, which was his responsibility.[42]

A battery of M18 Hellcats undertaking live ammunition practice firing during the manoeuvres in September 1953. (MCO)

Troops of the Fifth Military District wore German helmets, and were distinctive in this feature until the late 1950s. Here, seen during the manoeuvres in September 1953. (MCO)

Field Marshal Harding, Chief of the Imperial General Staff, was constantly present on the terrain where the manoeuvres were held, and he was Tito's personal guest for dinner on 23 September. Tito had visited the territory where the manoeuvres were held a number of times. According to public statements he was satisfied with the morale of the troops, especially the reserve conscripts.[43]

In the press conference held on 25 September 1953, the commander of the manoeuvres and the Fifth Military District, General Nadj, rejected the comments that the JNA manoeuvres were organized as a response to the deployment of the Italian troops on the Yugoslav border. Nadj, a former officer with the Spanish Republicans, said that the territory chosen bore witness that this was not a true, "besides, the manoeuvre was planned and prepared much earlier. There is no need to concentrate our troops on the Italian borders" he added. Most of the commentary on the manoeuvres was actually on the usage and adoption of the MDAP supplied equipment and weapons by the Yugoslav Army and on the morale of the troops.[44] This was repeated by Marshal Tito the following day, after the parade of the JNA troops that took part in the manoeuvre. According to his remarks, the Yugoslav Army had become the "modern, impregnable army of [a] socialist state."[45]

The Yugoslavs especially focused on the positive comments and remarks of the NATO guests after the exercises. They also carefully noted all of the positive reports in the press and media in the Allied and NATO states. The British press-agencies especially emphasised the positive comments and the impression of the JNA given by Field Marshal Harding. The American press in general was very enthusiastic and positive towards what the Yugoslav Army had shown at the manoeuvre and especially its usage of the MDAP – actually US – supplied weaponry.[46]

Field Marshal Montgomery addresses the Yugoslav press, Zagreb, September 1953. (MCO)

The Italian's were represented by Colonel Caliseo, the military attaché in Belgrade. According to the Yugoslav press, he commented positively on the cordial reception among his Yugoslav hosts, and showed admiration for what the Yugoslav soldiers demonstrated during the manoeuvres and stressed that he commented upon the exercises with the "eyes of the solider." On the contrary, the Italian press was very critical toward the Yugoslav exercises, commenting that their own journalists did not have the adequate conditions for objective insight. The Italians posed questions on the chosen timing

Old Trieste opponents: Marshal Tito and Field Marshal Harding exchanging opinions at the manoeuvres. Tito is surrounded by his generals: Nadj (CO Fifth Mil. District), Žeželj (Guards) and Gošnjak (Federal Defence Minister). (MCO)

General Nadj, commander of the Fifth Military District, exchanging views during the manoeuvres, with NATO representatives in September 1953. (MCO)

and place of the manoeuvres, concluding that they were no doubt linked with the rising tensions on the question of Trieste. They asked why Italian troops were not included in the exercises, commenting that the defence of such an important direction, in the case of aggression from the East, was not possible without the participation of the Italian Army.[47] It was actually true, but the manoeuvres were actually Tito's army's show and not an allied operation against possible eastern invaders.

After the parade held on 27 September 1953, all of the JNA units that had taken part in the manoeuvres started to return to their regular garrisons. In just ten days most of them would be activated gain, but now in different and much more serious circumstances.

4
EIGHTH OF OCTOBER 1953

The decision of the US and Great Britain to withdraw their forces from the city of Trieste and Zone A that surrounded the city, and to transfer the governing rights to Italy brought about an eruption in Yugoslavia that occurred on the 8 October 1953.[1] There is no written evidence that Marshal Tito had any information on what had been prepared among the Allies. His speeches in the meeting in Okruglica and Split in September may indicate that he anticipate such move and then decided to raise his stakes asking for a Yugoslav share in Zone A.

At 10:00 a.m. on that day, British Ambassador Ivo Mallet and *Charge d'Affaire* in the Belgrade US embassy Woodruff Wallner met Tito in his Belgrade office, and presented him with the joint decision of the US and British governments to withdraw troops from Zone A and hand authority to Italy.[2] The Allied diplomats explained to Tito that they counted on the Tito's verbal acceptance of such a division model which he exchanged with British Foreign Secretary Eden on 22 September 1952. The aim of this act was to downscale the tensions in the region and an improvement in the strategy of the defence of south-eastern Europe. It was a *de facto* solution which was intended to be final.[3]

Marshal Tito seen during the manoeuvres of September 1953. (MCO)

Tito was surprised but calm during the meeting. Most likely his pride was deeply hurt. To a journalist of the *Observer* he explained "Such kind of conduct hit me like out of the blue". Although, he added: "we were suspicious that behind the concentration of the Italian troops is hidden something in the back. The reason of our fear was the firm belief that such deployment of the Italian troops was not possible without the knowledge of the Allies, at least without their partial involvement." Although the meeting passed in a diplomatic tone,

Demonstrations in Belgrade against the Allied decision to withdraw its assets from Zone A and to give authority to Italy. (MCO)

Tito left with an "utmost heavy feeling" that this was an "ultimatum."[4] The Italians welcomed the news whilst describing Tito as *dittatore di Belgrado* – the dictator of Belgrade.[5]

On the evening of the reception held in the US Embassy in honour of General Vučković, Deputy of the Yugoslav General Staff who just arrived from constructive and successful negotiations in the United States, the atmosphere among the JNA top brass officers was grave. The public followed this pattern and tension rose.[6]

Yugoslav Forces on the Move towards Zone B and the Border

The Yugoslavs decided to act: to move their troops into Zone B and onto the border with Italy, and to threaten the Italians if their forces appeared in Zone A.

Within the Yugoslav General staff, all leave was cancelled and the number of the officers on duty within its departments and sections was increased. A task force named the *Operativna Grupa* (Operational Group) was ordered to be formed with its HQ in Postojna headed by General Kosta Nadj, commander of the Fifth Military District. The Operational Group was tasked to command the XXIII Corps and the bulk of forces consisted of mobilised divisions and brigades as well as the reinforcements from Fifth and Seventh Military Districts. Its main task was to prevent the entry of Italian forces into the city of Trieste.[7]

At 21:50 in the evening of 8 October, a phone rang in the office of the Yugoslav Navy *Eskadra* at that time in Pula. The order came that the *Eskadra* should be in Zone B's harbours by the morning. The order for movement, and combat instructions, were passed to the units and their ships in the following hour. The operational element of the *Eskadra* HQ boarded the destroyer *Triglav*, command vessel for the 6th Squadron. At 02:00 a.m. all of the *Eskadra*'s ships sailed for Zone B. There were four destroyers, eight patrol ships and 38 torpedo-boats, belonging to the 6th, 11th, 38th and 76th Squadrons assigned for this task. Four torpedo-boats of the 25th Guards Navy Detachment remained at combat readiness as the reserve in the Brioni Islands – Pula area.[8]

At dawn of 9 October, the ships of the *Eskadra* were deployed in combat readiness in the harbours of Zone B. 6th Destroyer Squadron deployed to Koper (later moved to Piran), with 38th Patrol Boat Squadron in the harbours of Koper and Izola, 11th Torpedo Boat Squadron in Umag and Novigrad, 76th Torpedo Borat Squadron in Poreč and vessels belonging to the *Eskadra* HQ in Piran. The Yugoslav Navy was welcomed in the cities of the Slovenian Littoral with enthusiasm. Citizens flocked around the ships carrying flowers and other gifts for the seamen. Among the crews the combat spirit was tremendous.[9]

At the same time the 1st Proletarian Division received the order to enter Zone B to strengthen the JNA *Odred* there. The division's elements were based in the wider area that surrounded Trieste from the Yugoslav side, which ranged 20-30 kilometres from the city. 3rd Proletarian Infantry Regiment was in Sent Peter/Pivka, 13th Proletarian Infantry Regiment in Ajdovščina, 106th Infantry Regiment in Vipava and 155th Artillery Regiment and other divisional

A courier on a Moto Guzzi motorcycle receiving orders during the first night of the Crisis, 8-9 October 1953. (MCO)

Yugoslav torpedo-boats in Zone B, mid-October 1953. (MCO)

Torpedo-boats of the 76th Torpedo Boat Squadron, Koper, October 1953. (MCO)

Alerted Yugoslav troops on the morning of 9 October 1953. (MCO)

A horse-drawn anti-tank battalion rushes towards the border on 9 October 1953. (MCO)

units were in Postojna.[10] "The trumpeter signalled the alarm, while the officer of the day was standing next to him. The ninth of October started. We jumped into the lorries…" was how one of the conscript solider of the 155th Artillery Regiment remembered events. The previous night, soldiers of the regiment were painting the slogans "*Tukaj smo Slovenci!* – Here are the Slovenes!" in red paint all over the walls towards the Italian and FTT borders. The division's units entered Zone B or deployed closer to the Italian border.[11] Those scenes were characteristic for many of the garrisons in the Fifth Military District in Slovenia and parts of Croatia.

The units of the XI and XXIII Corps and especially of the 20th Tank Division were alerted and moved out of their garrisons. The tank brigades of the 20th Division moved to the border: 232nd from Jastrebarsko (south from Zagreb in Croatia), 268th in Vrhnika (at the road Ljubljana-Trieste).[12] The third brigade of the division: the 265th – was stationed in Ilirska Bistrica and the small town of Podgrad, at the road which led from Rijeka to Trieste and was the closest tank brigade to Trieste. Its Sherman tanks moved in the early morning of 9 October towards Zone B. The young Second Lieutenant (later General) Milisav Djordjević, at that time a company commander in the 265th Brigade had been woken previously by the courier, who just said "Signal Wolf! Signal Wolf!" and rushed to wake the other officers in the town. "My God, it was very tough!" Djordjević recalled. He took his soldiers to the garages, where they loaded the Shermans with live munitions. They started movement to the village of Kozina at the border, where the Shermans took positions overlooking the city of Trieste. During the afternoon, plans and maps of Trieste were brought.

The commanders were given orders as to which direction and street they would advance along into the city.[13]

During 9 October commanders of the Fifth Military District, the *Eskadra*, 1st Proletarian Division and JNA *Odred* in Zone B met at Socerb castle, just above the Baia di Muggia, overlooking Trieste. They discussed the situation and the coordination of mutual actions.[14] The commander of the Yugoslav Military Authorities in Zone B of the FTT, Colonel Milos Stamatović, was summoned to Belgrade for consultations with the military top brass during the night 8-9 October. He returned back on the following day to Koper, "the capital of Zone B STT" as it was announced in the *Borba* daily.[15]

The II Intelligence Department of the Yugoslav General Staff established a task group with the assignment to gather and monitor information, maintain working maps together with the I Operational Department and maintain contact with all relevant institutions in the state. The Chief of the Intelligence Department and officers from the task group daily briefed the Yugoslav Minister of Defence and the Chief of the General Staff, and occasionally other top brass in the Yugoslav General staff. The Intelligence Department of the General Staff established contact with the foreign intelligence service (SID) as well as the State Security (UDBA) to exchange information from the intelligence centres and Yugoslav diplomatic representatives. Within the HQ of the Operational Group in Postojna, the Intelligence Group was formed. It was tasked to gather information on the ground and pass it to the Operational Group, Fifth Military District and the parent II Department in the General Staff. Yugoslav intelligence also relied on obtaining information through the existing chain

Yugoslav soldiers pulling an M1 57mm anti-tank gun on the morning of 9 October 1953. (MCO)

Soldiers preparing an M18 Hellcat, a US-made high speed tank destroyer armed with a 76mm gun. October 1953. (MCO)

Loaded on the train here are brand-new US-made M47 tanks of the 268th Tank Brigade. (MCO)

A self-propelled howitzer battalion moves to the border: column of M7 105mm Gun Motor Carriages headed by an M3A1 acting as a command vehicle. (MCO)

Yugoslav troops taking position, with villagers passing by to their regular field work. (MCO)

of reconnaissance, radio-surveillance and aviation reconnaissance units, as well as the military representative in Rome and a number of agents in northern Italy.[16] The specific problem for the Yugoslav military representatives was constant monitoring by the Italian security service and the limitation of movements to the city of Rome. Yugoslav military diplomats could only gather indirect information from the media and other military representatives in the Italian capital.[17]

On 15 October, Western press agencies (UP) noted the movement of an armoured brigade equipped with M47 Patton tanks through Postojna. Those were the tanks of the 268th Brigade from Vrhnika. Those first-line units were followed by other units from the garrisons in Slovenia. Motorised and artillery columns headed for the Slovenian Littoral, Istria and Western Slovenia. The units which remained in the garrisons, the second echelon, carried out the removal of equipment and ammunition from storage between 9 and 13 October. The Yugoslav daily *Borba* confirmed on 11 October that "reinforced contingents of the JNA units entered Zone B." This sudden movement was explained as being needed to stop the "provocations which lasted so far."[18] There were units from XI Corps which also headed to Trieste, such as the units of 56th Infantry Division: a battalion from the 55th Artillery Regiment deployed to Črni Kal south-east from the Trieste, while the 56th AA Artillery Battalion headed for Postojna.[19]

Various Western press agencies reported on the massive movements of the Yugoslav Army towards Trieste. Some of those reports provided details such as the visit of General Nadj and Admiral Černi to troops in Zone B. Others noted the positions of Yugoslav troops in Zone B, the border area and on the roads that headed inland to the area of Trieste. Both, Italian and Allied press agencies commented on the numbers of the engaged Yugoslav troops. Depending upon the agency or the magazine, those numbers ranged from 16,000 to 27,000, or by engaged divisions it ranged from five (AFP), to 8-10 (*The Times*) to 13 (*DPA, Corriere de Trieste*). According to reports of the AFP, the Yugoslavs were reinforcing their troops "without rush."[20] Members of the American Military Assistance Staff deployed to Yugoslavia, also monitored the movements of Tito's forces.[21]

To strengthen the units in Slovenia, the 252nd Tank Brigade was deployed from Kragujevac in Serbia. The brigade, equipped with Soviet T-34 tanks, was treated as the Supreme Command Reserve. Its tanks became stuck in mud while moving from their garages to the railway station. Under orders from General Jakšić, the commander of the First Military District, the tankmen cut branches from the nearby woods and managed to get the tanks out of the mud and loaded onto the trains. At 05:00 a.m. next morning, standing at Belgrade railway station, General Jakšić saluted the brigade loaded on the trains and heading to Sežana in Slovenia.[22]

The deployment of the T-34 Brigade from eastern Yugoslavia was not just strengthening the armoured units of the Fifth Military District but also a political move by Tito, according to Djilas' testimony. Milovan Djilas, at that time a member of the Central Committee of the Yugoslav Communist Party and later known worldwide for his opposition to Tito's rule, wrote, that Tito explained to him that it was "not convenient" to send the "American tanks" to Trieste, since US troops were based in the city.[23]

The Yugoslav Army forces which were moving to their positions were cheered by the

A column of GMC lorries headed by a single Dodge ambulance in the vicinity of Zone B. (MCO)

Soviet-built ZIS 76mm AT gun towed by US supplied GMC lorries arrived at their positions. (MCO)

Firing position of a 57mm AT gun. (MCO)

In the trenches: Yugoslav soldiers with distinctive German helmets at the edge of Zone B. (MCO)

crowds of the people with cheering and slogans typical for the time. Such an atmosphere was perceived as improving the morale of the troops.[24]

As the Yugoslav press and news agencies reported, on the very first day when the Yugoslav units entered Zone B, a stream of volunteers appeared at the military-recruiting establishments organized with the Association of the People's Liberation Struggle Veterans in the communities of Zone. On 13 October its number had risen to 4,000 men in Koper and on 16 October around 3,000 in Buje in Zone B. *Borba* proudly commented that every tenth citizen of Zone B was listed as a potential volunteer. What was unusual in the reports of the *Narodna armija* was the insistence that "large number of Italians also volunteered."[25] The radio of the Yugoslav military government in Zone B reported on 15 October that the first volunteer battalion formed in Koper consisted of 430 men from a total of 5,300 enlisted volunteers.[26]

Although the mobilisation was later remarked upon as being one of the problematic points for the JNA troops engaged in the Crisis, based upon the available facts it appears to have been successful since the reservists were recalled *en masse*. In the 32nd Aviation Division, 160 reservists reported from 167 called up on 15 October. It was a much better percent than achieved in the previous large manoeuvres held in September. Discipline was much better than in normal times. "Feeling is tremendous in the unit. Moral is at high level. Everyone wishes to fight with the Italians…" was noted in the operational diary of the division on 12 October.[27] Combat morale was also high among the crews of the *Eskadra*. The general feeling among the sailors was "very offensive" and the commander was obliged to instruct to "work carefully and not make foolish moves!" The warships in Zone B's harbours were cheered by the local population and the Yugoslav naval units established contact with local and political organisations which was described as "very close." [28]

Yugoslav Air Force on Alert

The III Air Corps with its HQ in Zagreb controlled western parts of Yugoslavia. It had three aviation divisions deployed in Zagreb-Pleso (32nd Division), Cerklje (37th Division), Pula and Zadar-Zemunik (21st Division) air bases. It had around the 240 aircraft on its strength. On its territory, at the Ljubljana-Polje air base was the Higher Aviation Officers School with the 185th Aviation regiment and around 40 piston-engined Yak-3, Yak-9P and S-49C fighters. At the time of the outbreak of the crisis the III Air Corps did not have a single jet engine aircraft.[29]

At 00:10 a.m. on the night of 8-9 October the Zagreb-based 32nd Division was alerted by phone calls from the Corps HQ. Couriers headed into the city to wake up and gather the flying and technical crews. The first group of airmen arrived at the air base at 02:15 a.m. The delays were mostly caused by young and inexperienced drivers not knowing city of Zagreb well. Ground crews started to disperse the division's Mosquitoes and to prepare the runaway and aprons. The communication officers started to establish the connection between the division's units and with other III Air Corps units. The 32nd Division was at Combat Readiness No. 3 – i.e. ready for action with at least 10 minutes notice – while each of the regiments maintained a pair at Combat Readiness No. 2 – ready to take off in just 5-10 minutes.[31]

37th Division at Cerklje air base was in a similar situation. During the night, technical crews prepared the F-47D Thunderbolts of the 111th Regiment and the obsolete Il-2 Shturmoviks of the 96th and 138th Regiments. Later, the ground crews managed to repair and return to availability a certain number of previously withdrawn

Table 10: III Air Corps Yugoslav Air Force Operational Strength During the Trieste Crisis[30]

Parent unit	Unit	Air base	Aircraft type – number available/serviceable	
			11 November 1953	1 December 1953
III Air Corps	Liaison Flight III AC	Zagreb-Borongaj	Oxford 1/1 Anson 1/1 PO-2 2/2 Fi-156 2/2 Zlin-381 2/2	Oxford 1/1 Anson 1/1 PO-2 2/2 Fi-156 2/2 Zlin-381 2/2
	Liaison Flight Fifth Military District	Zagreb-Borongaj	KAB Fazan 7/6 PO-2 2/1 Fi-156 2/2	KAB Fazan 7/7 PO-2 2/1 Fi-156 1/0
	184th Recce Aviation Regiment	Zagreb-Pleso	Mosquito NF.Mk 38 24/20 PO-2 1/1	Mosquito NF.Mk 38 32/27 PO-2 1/1
Attached from VII Air Corps	Squadron /103rd Recce Aviation Regiment	Zagreb-Pleso (home base: Batajnica)	Mosquito NF.Mk 38 (10 deployed)	Mosquito NF.Mk 38 (10 deployed)
Attached from 44th Division VII Air Corps	117th Fighter Aviation Regiment	Zagreb-Pleso (home base: Batajnica)	F-84G Thunderjet (14 deployed)	F-84G Thunderjet (14 deployed)
Higher Air Officers School	185th Aviation Regiment	Ljubljana Polje (moved to Pula)	Ikarus S-49C 28/23 plus number of other obsolete Yak3/9P fighters and trainers	Ikarus S-49C 28/26 plus number of other obsolete Yak 3/9P fighters and trainers
21st Aviation Division	HQ Detachment	Zadar-Zemunik	F-47D 3/3 Mosquito FB.Mk 6 2/2 Harvard 1/1 Me-109G 1/0 Oxford 1/1 PO-2 5/5 Fi-156 2/1	Mosquito FB.Mk 6 1/1 Mosquito FB.Mk 3 1/1 PO-2 3 /3
	97th Aviation Regiment	Zadar-Zemunik	Mosquito FB.Mk 6 18/18 Mosquito FB.Mk 3 2/1	Mosquito FB.Mk 6 21/15
	172nd FB Aviation Regiment	Zadar-Zemunik Pula (det.)	F-47D 23/21	F-47D 25/20
	122nd Seaplane Flight	Divulje naval air base	Sealand 2/1 Aero 2H 4/4	Sealand 2/2 Aero 2H 4/3
32nd Aviation Division	HQ Detachment	Zagreb-Pleso	Mosquito NF.Mk 38 2/0 Mosquito FB.Mk 6 7/5 Mosquito FB.Mk 3 4/4 PO-2 3/3	Mosquito FB.Mk 6 1/1 Mosquito FB.Mk 3 1/1 PO-2 3 /3
	88th Bomber Aviation Regiment	Zagreb-Pleso	Mosquito FB.Mk 6 18/14	Mosquito FB.Mk 6 19/13
	109th Bomber Aviation Regiment	Zagreb-Pleso	Mosquito FB.Mk 6 15/11	Mosquito FB.Mk 6 19/12
37th Aviation Division	HQ Detachment	Cerklje	PO-2 3 UT-2 3 Fi-156 1 Harvard 1	F-47D 1/1 Harvard 2/2 PO-2 3/2 UT-2 5/5 Fi-156 1/0
	111th FB Aviation Regiment	Cerklje	F-47D 21/20	F-47D 20/16
	96th Strike Aviation Regiment	Cerklje	IL-2 2 5/16 UIL-2 8/4	IL-2 18/13 UIL-2 5/4
	138th Strike Aviation Regiment	Cerklje	IL-2 22/15 UIL-2 8/4	IL-2 20/15 UIL-2 3/2
Attached from 21st Division	83rd FB Aviation Regiment	Cerklje (home base: Pula)	F-47D 21/21	F-47D 21/20

Group of soldiers laying anti-tank mines. (MCO)

Yugoslav soldiers in camouflage smocks posing with local children. (MCO)

A patrol on the move through a hamlet in Zone B, with a panorama of Trieste in the background. (MCO)

Inside one propaganda section officers prepare a bulletin for the troops. (MCO)

Young volunteers from Zone B at the start of their short military training. (MCO)

Shturmoviks and to create a divisional reserve nicknamed the 139th Regiment.[32] As the division was obviously a technically weak unit, YAF HQ decided to add another F-47D Thunderbolt regiment to Cerklje. The 83rd Regiment, which was based at Pula, was ordered to move to Cerklje and strengthen the 37th Division. The 21st Division dispatched a flight of F-47D to Pula from the Zadar based 172nd Regiment as a replacement. This division's 97th Regiment had Mosquito NF.Mk.38 and FB.Mk.VIs and the remaining Thunderbolts of the 172nd Regiment at high readiness.[33]

The 34th Air Zone was responsible for the air-technical maintenance and logistics of the III Air Corps' units. Its air bases, workshops, storage, AA artillery and engineer battalions were also alerted during the night of 8-9 October.[34] On the same night, the 105th Aerial Surveillance Battalion was activated and sent from Zagreb to the Nova Gorica area. Two days later, its HQ reported that the radar operational centre, radar and visual observing stations had been established. The battalion however, could only identify and note the violation of Yugoslav air space, any link with the fighter aviation would only be established in the years to come.[35]

As pointed out: the Yugoslav III Air Corps did not have any jet ircraft. On the other side of the border, the cutting edge of the Italian Air Force was three aviation brigades (5th, 6th and 51st) which were numerically comparable with the YAF divisions, but completely equipped with around 180 F-84G Thunderjets. Those brigades were based at Verona-Villafranca, Ghedi-Montichiari and Aviano. The advantage of the Italian Air Force was more than obvious.[36]

Up to the outbreak of the Trieste Crisis, the YAF had received a total of 54 Republic F-84G Thunderjets, with the first batch delivered to Yugoslavia on 9 June 1953 under the MDAP. Further deliveries continued in smaller or larger batches until the beginning of

October 1953. The two aviation regiments in Batajnica (117th and 204th) were in the middle of conversion to the type, and far from initial combat capability.[37] Despite that fact, sending the jets to the crisis zone in the west of Yugoslavia was necessary. The YAF HQ ordered that the partly converted 117th Regiment should be deployed to Zagreb-Pleso air base, subordinate to III Air Corps. On 14 October, 14 Thunderjets of the regiment landed at Zagreb-Pleso air base and two days later, the Thunderjets started with flying from this base.[38] Their flypast over Cerklje air base caused panic and surprise among the pilots and technicians of the F-47D and Il-2 equipped 37th Aviation Division as they thought that the Thunderjets belonged to the Italian Air Force and had caught them by surprise.[39]

Line-up of MDAP-supplied Mosquito FB Mk VI of the 32nd Aviation Division, Zagreb-Pleso air base. (M. Micevski collection)

F-47D Thunderbolts were also delivered through MDAP. This line-up is from the 111th FB Aviation Regiment, 37th Aviation Division at Cerklje air base. (MCO)

Thunderbolts of the 83rd FB Regiment at Cerklje, having arrived from Pula, 13 October 1953. (M. Micevski collection)

Prior to deployment, a YAF HQ commission analysed the level of combat readiness achieved in the 117th Regiment. It was noted that the conversion had achieved only fighter training at the level of four-ship detachments and only a few gunnery exercises and 50kg cement-bomb drops had been carried out at the Čenta range. After the arrival at Pleso, gunnery practice was continued using aerial "sausage" targets towed by Thunderbolts, and with live firing of the HVAR 5-in rockets carried out at the temporary range at Crna Mlaka, south of Zagreb. These were new experiences for the pilots of the regiment, "we had the airplanes with radar and gyroscope sights. No one among the pilots didn't know how to use the sight. We also had minor knowledge in firing manoeuvres, too", remembered pilot Predrag Vulić.[40]

The 117th Regiment was tasked with air-defence of Zagreb and the wider area of the western Yugoslav skies. The runaway at Pleso was immediately lengthened by 200 metres at either end to enable the Thunderjets adequate landing and taking-off conditions. A team from the YAF HQ was later despatched to investigate which parts of the Belgrade-Zagreb motorway would be suitable for Thunderjets to operate from in case of the widening of the conflict with Italy.[41]

A technician of the 37th Division writing slogans in chalk on an obsolete, but combat ready Il-2 Shturmovik. (M. Micevski collection)

The Thunderjet pilots of the 117th Regiment grew moustaches to distinguish themselves from other units while deployed at Pleso. (Predrag Vulić)

Friuli, alongside the border with Yugoslavia and the FTT were ready for instant deployment.

On 10 October, the Italian General Staff ordered the deployment of the divisions *Trieste* and *Cremona* towards the border with Yugoslavia, while the overall command of the forces that were ordered to intervene in Zone A was subordinated to V Corps. The earlier plan for intervention in Zone A (15 September 1953), was now changed in some details, excluding the usage of paratroopers for example, and considered two scenarios, one with Yugoslav political acceptance and the one without it.

The Deputy of the Italian Chief of the General Staff commented that this plan was aggressive, pointing out that in the case of a mutual entry into Zone A, the flow of events of could not be controlled and full scale hostility could result from some trivial incident. Such a scenario was not wanted either by the Italians nor by the Yugoslavs, and it could harm the local Italian population. The Chief of the Operations Department in the Italian General Staff went to Trieste on the 15 October to appraise the situation and try to establish contact with the Allied occupation force, but the Allies refused any contact.

On 16 October, the Italian Ministry of Defence enabled the mobilisation of a further 3,000 men to fill out the *Cremona, Legnano, Mantova, Folgore, Ariete* and *Centauro* divisions. Division *Trieste* was reinforced by adding infantry companies extracted from the 9th, 13th and 60th Infantry Regiments.

In response to the large deployment of the Yugoslav Army on the border with Italy and Zone B, the Italian government decided to close the border crossings and to evict the part of the population in the border area. These measures had been partly launched and carried out since 13 September as a pre-emptive measure, but now, it was a much more serious situation.

The deployment of the Italian V Corps included the division of the front-line (marked by the border with Yugoslavia and Zone B) into three zones:

- northern part, from Tarvisio and below controlled by Division *Julia*,

L' esigenza T (Trieste) – Movements and Activities of the Italian Army[42]

After the Allied decision to hand over responsibility in Zone A to Italy, the Chief of the Italian General Staff ordered preparations for deployment by the V Corps and it subordinated units. Those included mostly armoured units: Armoured Division *Ariete*, Light Armoured Regiment *Genova*, self-propelled artillery, motorised elements of the Infantry Division *Folgore*, parts of the Regiment *Novara* and also Division *Trieste* as the reinforcement.

On the following day, the Italian General staff estimated that replacement of the Allied forces by the Italians in Zone A should be made without hurry. The main unit which would carry this plan, *Delta*, would be V Corps. Part of this unit which was stationed in

- middle part, around Gorizia with Division *Mantova* responsible,
- southern part in Crasso/Kras sector with Division *Folgore*.

The Armoured Division *Ariete* was held in the reserve of the V Corps, while two howitzer regiments were tasked to provide fire support for the whole front-line.

Both sides armed: the view from the Yugoslav to Italian side in the divided city of Gorizia, October 1953. (MCO)

Italian troops were tasked to monitor the border together with the interior force, then to take up positions for defence in the case of eventual attack. By using the natural advantages of the border, the defence should be effective with the usage of armour and motorised forces. In the case of a Yugoslav attack, the supply lines for their troops would be attacked and/or blocked. Part of the border area was mined and the vital roads which led from Carsso into the deeper Italian lands were blocked with anti-tank obstacles.

General Biglino, commander of V Corps decided to mobilise the *Taurinese* Brigade and to move Alpine Brigade *Tridentina* into the area around the city of Gemona on 18 October. He also requested assistance in deployment of the Forward Air Controller/Tactical Air Control Party elements to V Corps. As the general crisis did not show any sign of calming down, the Italian General staff enabled another mobilisation of 10,000 reservists on 19 October to fill out parts of *Friuli* and *Legnano* Divisions, as well as two battalions of the Alpine Brigade *Cadore*. More troops were sent to the north-east: a self-propelled rtillery unit from *Cremona* Division was send via railway to Pordenone, *Taurinese* Brigade to the area of Osoppo and *Orobica* Brigade to the Pusteria Valley.

In the same period, the Italian Naval Group Adriatic was strengthened by the introduction of three more corvettes and one submarine, on 18 October. These remained in their regular locations, but at a higher state of alert. One week later, six more ships were available in their parent harbours (they had earlier been undergoing repairs). A training sailing ship, *Vespucci*, was also added to the available list.

The Italian General Staff estimated that the ammunition supplies necessary for the deployed units on the north-eastern borders were generally low. The available quantities were critical for the 12.7mm heavy machineguns, 81mm mortars, 88mm Bazookas and recoilless guns. Ammunition was also deficient for 60mm mortars and generally low for the howitzers. By the beginning of November, the General Staff ordered that the lack of the ammunition should be solved with the organisation of supply units for the whole V Corps.

Another variation of the Italian Army operations plan was finished on 20 October. The main task was the occupation of Zone A. It was planned that the task should be carried out by the Division *Trieste* supported by the infantry and artillery regiment from *Cremona* Division, a single *Carabinieri* mobile battalion, a light armoured regiment, an armoured group, a *Bersaglieri* battalion and finally the Battalion *San Marco*. The reinforced *Trieste* Division would be organised into five tactical groups, among them one consisting of *Bersaglieri* and *Carabinieri* would land from the sea, while one would remain as the reserve. The whole *Cremona* Division was ordered to deploy south of the city of Udine, while the movement of the *Taurinese* Division was suspended.

On 24 October the Italian General Staff decided to reinforce the air defence of the AM bases in Aviano, Treviso, Vicenza, Ghedi and Villafranca with AA batteries, most likely as a result of information on the strengthening the Yugoslav Air Force capacities with Thunderjets and reconnaissance sorties inside Italian territory. The completion of the three groups of AA artillery for the defence of the territory (DAT – *Difensa Antiaerei Territoriale*) was also ordered. These were tasked to defend the railway junction in Bologna and two important bridges on the Po River. In the south, around Rome, the 1st Group of DAT was activated to protect the capital. Finally, upon the request of the V Corps commander, on 25 October, the V Communications Battalion was organised in Padova, tasked to co-operate with the AM units.

On 26 October, commander of the V Corps – General Biglino – informed his superiors that he had decided to open the border crossings to Yugoslavia for political reasons, and to keep them open. Moreover, on the 6 November, Biglino allowed regular leave for his troops, but not to exceed 15 percent of the effective strength of the units.

During November 1953, the Italian Army continued to reinforce the units near Yugoslavia and Zone B. On 9 November, the Alpine Brigade *Cadore* was moved into the front line. The V Corps reserve in that period consisted of *Ariete* and *Cremona* Division and *Tridentina* Brigade, tasked to carry out counter-attacks and to maintain the last defences on the Natsione, Torre and Isonzo Rivers. On 10 November the commander of the corps agreed to the laying of anti-tank mines on the roads which may be used by the advancing Yugoslavs if needed.

Challenge for Yugoslav Intelligence: Monitoring the Italian Movements

The Yugoslavs carefully monitored the deployments and movements of the Italian Army during the Trieste Crisis. Its official daily *Borba* had since 11 October reported on the Italian movements, and those had indicated that reinforcements were arriving from the border with the FTT all the way up to the Austrian border. The armoured units had been spotted on 13 October on the border with Zone A, and on 19 October around Gorizia. Allegedly, disguised officers of the *Mantova* Division were already in the city of Trieste. There had been violations of Yugoslav air space on 12 and 13 October and incidents such as the illumination of the Yugoslav side with searchlights (13 October). In other cases, the Yugoslav press noted movements and reinforcements on either side of the border.

Regardless of press reports, it was soon discovered that the Intelligence Group attached to the HQ in Postojna did not have any particular experience in operational work in the field. Gathering of information started by simply using the existing observation towers or watch posts that were near the border line. A radio-surveillance element was formed within the Intelligence Group which monitored the whole of the Italian radio-traffic in north-eastern Italy. Later, the radio surveillance started to bear fruitful results, since the radio-communication had doubled on the Italian side. A lack of Italian radio-discipline enabled the Yugoslavs to obtain much precise information on the Italian deployment.[43]

The Yugoslav agents who operated on Italian territory monitored the activities of V Corps in the wider area neighbouring Trieste and Gorizia. Others who were deeper in Italian territory received the task of monitoring the movements of other Italian army corps as well as activities in the AM bases in Verona, Vicenza, and elsewhere. After the crisis it was estimated that those agents managed to "establish control" over the movements of the Italian forces, but the results in gathering facts and figures where "modest."

Yugoslav military intelligence soon learned the difficulties of countering disinformation efforts that were "skilfully launched" by the Italian military intelligence. After the crisis, it was concluded that the Italian Army did not mobilize or create new units, rather they had filled-out the existing units in north-eastern Italy with reserve personnel. To create the notion of a massive deployment and concentration towards Yugoslavia, the Italian Army carried out false movements of its troops and had spread disinformation. During the crisis the frequent movements of armoured and motorised units from Udine and Portogruaro towards Gorizia and Gradisca were discovered and monitored. Information on the movements were received daily. The first Yugoslav estimation was that the *Ariete* Armoured Division was moving from the Sacile-Pordenone area towards the border. That news was soon to be denied once it was discovered that the complete division remained in its garrisons. The Yugoslavs supposed after that that this was the *Centauro* Armoured Division from III Corps which was deploying to the border but it was soon discovered that the *Centauro* Division was also still in its regular garrisons.

The movements of the Italian troops continued, and these started to worry Yugoslav intelligence, already counting hundreds of Italian vehicles in the vicinity of the border. Military intelligence established contacts with Yugoslav State Security and they finally discovered the Italian deception. Through night observation, they soon discovered that the vehicles seen on the roads during the day heading from west (Udine, Pordenone) to east (Gorizia, Gradisca) were returning overnight in the opposite direction. It was finally discovered that there were no other armoured vehicles in addition to those which were already in the area assigned to *Mantova* Division and the light armoured regiment. These were constantly cruising by day and night to create the impression of a large deployment and a rise in the number of armoured vehicles in the border area. The Yugoslav intelligence department suggested that the Operational Department of the General Staff organize the same kind of false operation. The idea was accepted but since the crisis began to calm down, the idea was abandoned.

Another case illustrates a lack of knowledge which led to a completely wrong conclusion. During October, Yugoslav border units reported several motorized columns approaching Trieste noted as entering Zone A and presumed that these were Italian forces. The HQs of the XXIII Corps and Yugoslav *Odred* in Zone B were alarmed. The news was passed to the Intelligence Group, which managed to check the information at nigh time and dawn. It was discovered that the motorized columns seen entering Zone A actually belonged to a battalion of the US 351st Infantry Regiment returning from exercises held in Western Germany. If the information from the border guards had been taken for granted, it could have resulted in serious problems. Such examples show the challenges for Yugoslav intelligence during the Trieste crisis.[44]

A platoon of the Yugoslav 345th Mountain Brigade prior to movement to the border area. (MCO)

It is obvious that some of the facts and figures published in the Yugoslav newspapers were done so with the intention of showing the pressure from the Italian Army. In other cases, the information was no doubt an outcome of the Italian deception operation to lead the Yugoslavs to believe that they had deployed far more troops than they actually had. Finally, most of the reports were intended to show low morale on the part of the Italian troops. During the crisis, the Yugoslav press often made parallels with the Italian Army during the Second World War and the occupation of Yugoslavia in 1941-1943. On the contrary, the positive morale of the deployed JNA units and warm welcome of the Slovene inhabitants was constantly illustrated.[45]

Italian Estimations of the Yugoslav Army

No matter the attempts of the Yugoslav media to denigrate Italian morale, their army was actually a respectable opponent, well equipped and backed by the Allies in this matter. Allied military representatives visited different Italian units deployed in the border area on 27 October.

According to the Italian documents, British and American officers commented that "many things were done, but not enough. [Italian troops] should be able to intervene fast, but without provoking incidents. [Italian] troops left good impression." In other visits by the Allied officers, the Italians noted that one American major praised the Yugoslav use of M47 Patton tanks.

On 25 October the Italian General Staff produced a comparative study of Italian and Yugoslav forces. It was concluded that Yugoslav forces were numerically stronger, deployed in the field – though not in fortified positions – and able to conduct a sustained advance deep into Italian areas. Yugoslav forces were "Seemingly in aggressive spirit", but it was noted that a serious examination showed weakness in Yugoslav cohesion. The report considered the defence and mobilisation potentials of the both nations. The mobilisation reserves favoured Italy and were far superior to those of Yugoslavia. The population was 3:1 in favour of Italy and the Italian army was described as well trained and with modern equipment.[46]

"Never more under Italy!" a GMC truck, loaded with troops, passing unde a slogan that summarized the feelings of the Slovene inhabitants in Zone B and border areas. (MCO)

Except for the youngest generations of conscript soldiers, the Yugoslav reserve forces were trained on the common military equipment and mostly trained to fight in the guerrilla fashion. The Italian General Staff estimated that the "low cultural level of the Yugoslav population" remains as a problem for establishment of larger numbers of the various specialists needed for a modern force. However, it was remarked that "Yugoslav war industry manages, with difficulties, to fulfil all the needs of its armed forces". A second analysis of the Yugoslav side, dated in the first half of November provided in-depth review of the interior situation in Yugoslavia, focusing on the economic problems. Analysing the armed forces, the Italians noted that after the first days of Yugoslav euphoria, the morale of the troops started to decline and that difficulties in logistics were seen, including the lack of food. Italian estimations indicated that most of the JNA units in Zone B were "reliant on local resources" and that lack of winter gear and fuel is evident. All of these shortcomings resulted in a "fall of discipline and feeling of military responsibility in general, desertion and absence without official leave coupled with not replying to mobilisation calls." Whilst the criticism in general seemed to be true there were no listed examples to demonstrate such conclusions.

By the beginning of November, the Yugoslav press still maintained the image of an atmosphere of fear and difficulties among the Italian troops. *Borba* and *Narodna armija* constantly created such images, quoting – or inventing – numerous examples to show that Italian troops were not willing to fight and that they had poor morale. One Italian solider who defected to the Yugoslav side at the end of October was regarded as the proof for the terrible situation among the Italian troops. His name was Antonio (Andrija) Korda, previously assigned to the 114th Infantry Regiment of the *Mantova* Division.[47] The Italian V Corps reported on 28 October to its General Staff that the soldier was missing from the outpost near Sabotin.[48] The testimony of this soldier immediately appeared in the Yugoslav press, and the official information from Korda's testimony was sent to the units of the JNA on 29 October to be read out to the personnel.[49]

While the Yugoslavs could praise the occasional desertions of Italian soldiers, deserters from their side caused more serious damage. In November, pilot Branislav Karić from the 97th Regiment at Zemunik-Zadar air base defected across the Adriatic and landed at the AM base in Ancona, and had allegedly taken sensitive documents and plans from his unit. Captain Nikola Žutić, commander of a squadron in the 103rd Reconnaissance Regiment was sent from Zagreb to Italy by train, to bring back Karić's Mosquito.[50]

At the Edge of Confrontation

Although the Trieste Crisis caused huge tensions and both sides carried out their tasks and deployments in much the manner that they would had war already started, there were no direct confrontations between the Yugoslav and Italian armies. There were, however, a series of incidents ranging from the violation of air space, to firing upon the other side, to occasional desertions.

According to the facts and figures revealed by the Italian V Corps on 16 November, in the previous period of the crisis there were two violations of the border on the ground, and over 10 violations of Italian airspace. Italian troops opened fire from their observation posts in four cases on "groups of unknown individuals."[51]

At the beginning of the Crisis, the Yugoslav Navy *Eskadra* was placed at combat readiness No. 1 – with complete crew and combat ready – which was later replaced by combat readiness No. 2 – where half of the crew was at action stations. The Yugoslav Navy carried out patrols at the edge of Yugoslav territorial waters. In the earlier phase of the crisis, the 38th Patrol Boat Squadron deployed three of its vessels near the city of Piran and at the capes of Savudrija and Debeli. From these positions they established control over the whole shore of Zone B. Each of the patrol boats would be given a position, and sailed without lights. At the ordered position they turned their engines off and remained in the dark, waiting in ambush. There were no serious incidents, however, other than the interception of several Italian fishing boats or US Navy vessels that sailed to or from Trieste. In November, a single US destroyer was intercepted in a show of force by two Yugoslav destroyers backed by several torpedo boats and even a detachment of Thunderbolts from Pula air base took-off.[52]

Units of the III Air Corps were also active. The backbone of the Yugoslav Air Force in the Trieste Crisis were four regiments with Mosquito NF.38 and FB.6 and three regiments with F-47D Thunderbolts. It was a formidable assault force which could deliver a considerable strike against Italian targets. Besides training in strike and fighter-bomber missions both types were used extensively for

Patrol boats of the *Kraljevica*-class belonging to the 38th Patrol Boat Squadron. (MCO)

The destroyer *Učka* on patrol. (MCO)

A pair of Thunderbolts belonging to 172nd FB Regiment were deployed to Pula and cooperated with the Yugoslav Navy along the Istrian shore. (Petar Novaković)

patrolling and cooperating with the Yugoslav Navy in the Adriatic.

Several exercises were held in the period of the crisis. Operating from Pula, the 172nd Regiment took part in an exercise with the navy in the Piran-Koper area (Zone B).[53] The largest tactical exercise of the III Air Corps was held on 10 November. The basic idea was to simulate a strike on the airfield near the city of Ajdovščina which acted as the enemy air base. The pilots of the 37th Division, with Thunderbolts, were successful, while the 32nd Division, with Mosquitos, failed in their attacks. The first group of the 88th Regiment did not manage to discover the well-hidden targets and returned back to Zagreb-Pleso without success. The other group violated Italian space by mistake, and their crews became the butt of jokes ("they went to buy stockings in Italy"[54]) from other pilots of the division. Earlier, on 21 October, 32nd Division was tested in a quick reaction alert. One section of four Mosquitos from 109th Regiment and pair from 88th Regiment were alerted from combat readiness No. 3. The test showed that it took 57 minutes from receiving the task to the take-off rather than the little over 10 minutes expected.[55]

YAF forward controllers deployed in the vicinity of Nova Gorica were tasked to guide strike aviation in the event of hostilities. (Ljubisa Ćurguz)

103rd Recce Regiment pilots of Mosquito NF 38s prepare for a sortie. (author's collection)

The 32nd Division mainly relied upon the Mosquito as it prime means of attack. It was in a constant struggle to maintain as many airframes as possible as serviceable. According to the Division's logbook the highest daily number reached during the crisis was 38 airworthy aircraft out of 46-49 available; usually it was 20+ airworthy Mosquitoes. This was surely the consequence of the intensive flying which ranged from 79 to 115 sorties per day. In the later phase of the crisis it was decided that operational resources should be better preserved: some of the aircraft were used for flying and training, while others were kept in the hangars, prepared for real combat use.[56]

Aerial Reconnaissance Missions

Both air forces, the Yugoslav JRV and Italian AM played a crucial role in the Trieste Crisis. In fact, they were the only part of either armed force to carry out their real combat mission: reconnaissance missions over the territory of other states.

The basic Yugoslav aerial reconnaissance platform was British-made MDAP-supplied Mosquito NF Mk 38. A total of 60 were assigned to the 103rd and 184th Reconnaissance Regiments, attached to each of the two Air Corps of the YAF, and to the 97th Bomber Regiment which operated a flight of this type tasked to cooperate with the navy over the Adriatic.

On 13 October, 184th Regiment moved from Cerklje to Pleso air base. It was engaged in reconnaissance and sideways photography of Italian border territory. This unit was able to carry out only daytime and tactical recce missions. As the need to obtain proper information on the movements and positions of the Italian forces grew daily, it was decided that reconnaissance assets should be strengthened. The

103rd Regiment Mosquitos taking off. (MCO)

Mosquito NF.38 serialed 8030/30 lands after a recce sortie. (M. Micevski collection)

103rd Regiment from Batajnica air base near Belgrade dispatched a squadron with ten Mosquito Mk 38s on 22 October to Pleso. The squadron remained independent and its usage was to be coordinated by the II Intelligence Section of the YAF HQ with the requests of the II Intelligence Department of the General staff. Since its establishment in May 1947, the 103rd Recce Regiment was regarded as the strategic reconnaissance asset of the YAF. It was the first unit which received MDAP-supplied Mosquitoes, while its airmen were trained by the RAF in 1951. The 103rd Regiment was a hub for all initial conversions to the Mosquito in 1952 as a result of which several of its pilots gained a large number of flying hours and experience in different flying conditions. In 1952-1953 the regiment reached full operational capability including carrying out the night recce missions.[57]

The squadron from 103rd Regiment immediately went into action. Its crews started with photographic reconnaissance missions inside Italian territory and over Zone A. The aim was to discover fortification works, artillery positions and mobilisation points. Higher authorities said of the missions that the "Gathered facts were very interesting." According to the recollections of Colonel Lipovšćak, who commanded the regiment, photo-materials were taken from the cameras, developed quickly and immediately sent to Belgrade for further analysis. Lipovšćak explained that some of the recce flights were carried out from Batajnica prior to movement to Zagreb. He photographed US Navy ships in Trieste harbour from 7,000 metres altitude, accompanied by a captain from Intelligence Department of the General Staff observing the mission.[58]

Most of the photo-reconnaissance missions were carried out by following the River Sava to the north-west, then entering Italian air space from the mountains of Austria at high altitude, or directly into Italian air space by flying low through Yugoslav air space and "jumping" to the necessary altitude for photography over Italy. The Yugoslav pilots flying Mosquitos managed to reach as far as Venice and the River Po. All of the pilots of the 103rd Regiment interviewed pointed out that the most spectacular reconnaissance-sortie was carried out not by their crews, but a crew from the 184th Regiment: pilot Captain Flajs and observer Captain Dimkovski. Their task was to discover and photograph object in the vicinity of Udine which were supposed to be a new AM air base. Two previous missions had failed. This crew managed to successfully carry out the mission, even taking photos twice from the extreme altitude of 10,000 metres. As a YAF official concluded "It showed that in the case of need, the reconnaissance aviation could be used as an additional but valuable way of gathering information."[59]

The HQ of V Corps counted ten Yugoslav violations of Italian air space between 19 October and 16 November.[60] The Italian Foreign Ministry officially protested to the Yugoslav side on 12 November on those intrusions of Italian air space. They noted some of the identified sorties of Yugoslav aircraft:

- 31 October, 11:05-11:15, Gorizia airfield, altitude 1,500 metres, Mosquito.
- 1 November, 12:25-12:35, Gorizia-Gradisca-Doberdob, altitude 300 metres, twin-engined aircraft.
- 1 November, 20:00-20:15, Gorizia
- 1 November, 21:15-21:30, Gorizia
- 2 November, 19:00-19:25, Foggia-Bari-Palese, altitude 2,000 metres
- 7 November, 10:35-10:45/four times, Udine, altitude 1,500 metres, Mosquito
- 11 November, 13:00-13.05, Valzone di Gorizia, altitude 1,500 metres, two twin-engined a/c

The Yugoslav Foreign Ministry asked the head of the II Intelligence

Department GS JNA to deny such accusations. It was explained that there were no such flights, since the YAF HQ strictly controlled flying in the border areas.[61]

A crew from the Postojna-based AA Artillery Battalion of the 1st Proletarian Division, late October 1953. (MCO)

Thunderjet "33" of the 117th Fighter Regiment returns from a sortie. (M. Micevski collection)

The Italian Air Force also carried out such intrusions and reconnaisance missions into Yugoslav air space. Their sorties were a serious challenge for the small and new aerial early warning service within the YAF. The Yugoslav press agency *TANJUG* reported that on the morning of 13 October four Italian aircraft violated Yugoslav airspace. The YAF radar network registered Italian aircraft on 17 October at 11:46 a.m. in the wider area Pula-Poreč. Two more violations were identified on 20 October, followed by violations on 22 and 23 October. On 23 October, radio-silence was ordered by the YAF HQ to avoid possible eavesdropping by the Italians. Further intrusions by Italian aircraft, resulted in an order being issued on 29 October that the ports of Pula, Poreč and others with Yugoslav warships, as well as all of the air bases within the territory of III Air Corps were not to be overflown by Yugoslav aircraft. This was a measure of precaution so that foreign aircraft could be identified much easier and to avoid the potential opening fire of the Yugoslav AA artillery upon its own aircraft.[62]

By the beginning of November, the Yugoslavs registered 23 Italian violations of their air space. Further intrusions followed in November. On 13 November four Italian aircraft entered Yugoslav air space in the area of Tolmin.[63] The first QRA response of the Yugoslav fighters occurred on 26 November. Upon receiving information that Italian aircraft had been spotted in Yugoslav air space, two F-84G Thunderjets took-off from Zagreb air base. It took nine minutes from signal to take-off. It was a major improvement over the previous exercise, although none of the Italian aircraft were seen upon arrival in the border area. It is worth noting that YAF HQ issued an order on 18 October, Italian aircraft caught in Yugoslav air space should not be fired upon unless fired at first.[64] The experience of shooting down two USAAF C-47s in 1946 in nearly the same area, was a good lesson for the Yugoslavs on how such a hasty reaction could complicate the international position of their state.

Allied Forces in the FTT and Trieste Crisis

After the escalation of the crisis, the Allies reacted with military-diplomatic pressure on Yugoslavia. Their main standpoint was the division of the FTT into two zones, Italian and Yugoslav. It was already perceived as a solution which would satisfy Yugoslavia nearly 100 percent and that there was no need to overreact with military force. Nobody among the politicians or military commanders in NATO was in favour of any kind of military action against Yugoslavia, but everyone was certain that a sudden crisis would harm the defence architecture of southern Europe.[65]

The Allied forces in the FFT at the time were under the command of the British General John Winterton. He was also military governor in the FTT, and had occupied this post since 1951. The Allied contingent consisted of the British 24th Brigade and the US 351st Infantry Regiment. Upon the decision by Italy to assume authority in Zone A, the Allied force would withdraw from the FTT.[66]

Immediately after the crisis started, Allied troops were seen patrolling the FTT boundaries and the military police were especially active, whilst for their part the Yugoslavs monitored Allied movements in and out of the FTT. Although active on the ground, the Allied forces were preparing to leave, as reported by the Routers news agency on 15 October. They were selling surplus equipment, evacuating stores and removing road signs. As the UPI press agency stated, the commander of the 3rd Battalion of the 351st Regiment, which was deployed on border of the FTT, claimed that his soldiers, among them many veterans from Korea were ready for action.[67] News agencies also reported on 27 October that 230 spouses and children of the British servicemen had already left Trieste, including the spouse of General Winterton.[68]

On 10th October three destroyers from the US 6th Fleet entered

A solider of BETFOR stands near a Land Rover with the insignia of 24th Brigade, at the Skofje border crossing between Zones A and B, 1954. (MCO)

Marshal Tito speaks to the gathered crowd, early October 1953. (author's collection)

A reconnaissance unit with distinctive smocks and German-style helmets on patrol in the Kras area, at the edge of Zone B. (MCO)

Trieste harbour. The squadron was commanded by Captain Freiburghaus. Although the Italian press speculated that this was in answer to the appearance of the Yugoslav Navy in Zone B, actually on 12 October two of the US destroyers left Trieste, leaving only USS *New* (DD-818) with the squadron commander.[69] On that very same day, 12 October, Vice Admiral Jearuld Wright, Commander-in-Chief of the US Naval Force Eastern Atlantic and Mediterranean, arrived in Belgrade upon the invitation of the Yugoslav Chief of the Defence, General Peko Dapčević. Wright, with his aides, remained as a guest for four days inspecting the units, academies and other establishments of the Yugoslav Navy. The visit coincided with the deployment of the Yugoslav Navy into Zone B, and the situation was most likely matter for discussion between the Americans and Yugoslavs.[70]

In an interview published on 16 October, Tito firmly stated that his troops would not fight against Allied forces in the FTT, but, he noted that if Italian troops entered Zone A under the protection of the Allied forces or under NATO cover, "it will have a catastrophic reaction in Yugoslavia."[71]

Sometime after the escalation of the Trieste Crisis the voices in the West commented that Tito's threats could influence the flow of economic and military assistance to Yugoslavia. Some of the congressmen that actively appeared in the American media asked that military aid to Yugoslavia should be stopped in reaction on the Trieste Crisis as well as President Eisenhower's announcement that military aid for Yugoslavia for another fiscal year would be US$216 million. Defence Secretary Charles Wilson stated that eventual termination of the military assistance to Yugoslavia was not related to the Trieste Crisis. The New York Times commented on the possibility that economic and military aid to Tito's Yugoslavia could stop if the crisis do not calm down. It was pointed out that Yugoslavia needed the United States much more than vice versa.[72]

In a speech during the massive meeting held in Leskovac, Tito commented: "Somebody in the West will say: "Here they are. See how they behave. And you should give them assistance!" Well, we are grateful for the assistance. We said that for [a] hundred times. But we cannot sell our land for that assistance. We cannot give out land soaked with blood for that assistance. It looks that way, and we do not want to be like that." Tito stressed "...than we refuse any assistance!"[73]

The 345th Mountain Brigade was deployed in the most northern and mountainous part of the Yugoslav-Italian border during the Trieste Crisis. (MCO)

The Supreme Allied Commander in Europe, General Alfred Gruenther, stated on 15 October in The Hague "that every conflict which escalates within NATO directly affects its members." This statement was direct confirmation that Yugoslavia at that moment was perceived as a NATO member. He added that he hoped that both states were "aware enough of the real freedom which exists from this side of the Iron Curtain". He stressed the importance of peace and hoped that Italy and Yugoslavia would not enter into open hostility.[74]

Much later, the Yugoslav daily *Borba* published on its front page "Is the Atlantic Pact's Supreme Command aware of what it is doing?" The anonymous author – signed as J.S. – criticised NATO and its supreme commander General Gruenther, saying that they were informed of the movement of the Italian Army troops since they were part of NATO. The author sharply noted that Italy was pushing NATO into "aggressive waters", and that NATO do not care much to supress Italian expansionism. The author appealed to NATO to understand the situation, so that it should avoid becoming the "instrument of expansion and aggression."[75]

Tito's Comments on the Crisis

Marshal Tito was notably sharp in his comments during the crisis to the Yugoslav public. In his speech at the huge meeting at Leskovac airfield in South Serbia on 10th October he explained: "Our troops were ordered to enter Zone B as the reinforcement for our detachment stationed there." On the following day in Skoplje, Macedonia, Tito stated: "I stress that we shall constantly monitor if any of the Italian soldiers will enter Zone A. The same moment if they enter, we will enter that zone!"[76]

In Skoplje, Tito explained the actions carried out by the JNA in the previous days: "We are criticised that we are threatening with the mass deployment of the troops. But we do nothing different than Italians have done [a] couple of months before, when they massed the troops on our borders. I have already said in [large meetings] in Okroglica and Split that we shall not react immediately by deploying our troops, since we treat it as comedy performed by their side. But, I said that we shall have a time to arrive there, if we estimate that [the] interests of our state are jeopardized. Now, the time has come, and we had to go there. Now, comrades, is the time when we had to do it, when he have to take all the necessary and legal precautions to stop the new treason over our state." Tito denied all of the foreign charges that Yugoslavs were "temperamental", "hasty" and "irreconcilable".[77]

Two weeks later, on 24 October, Tito commented to *France Press* that the concentration of troops was started by the Italian side, as he pointed out "with very dubious motivation that Yugoslavia allegedly wants to annex Zone B." Tito maintained the standpoint that the Yugoslav Army did not immediately start to deploy troops in response, to avoid disruption of mutual relations, no matter that it was the clear and planned move to apply "pressure on our country". The concentration of troops was carried out when it was clear that the Italians intended to occupy Zone A with the assistance of the Allies. "We have deployed our troops with the aim to stop such [a] violent act, [an] act of aggression against our land and interests. And second, to protect the inviolability of our territory in general." Tito stressed the firm standpoint that Yugoslav troops would enter Zone A if those territories were handed over to Italy.[78]

Djilas, our reliable first-hand witness, comments on Tito's behaviour way from the public appearances:

> Although Tito expressed general [Yugoslav] bitterness, in his decisions were deliberate stressing of the independence to the West, especially in the period when post-Stalin changes were indicated in the Soviet Union... I have asked him: How shall we fire upon Italians, when they are protected by the Americans and English? He said to me: If the Italians enter, we will enter too. And we shall see...[79]

5
TOWARDS THE COMPROMISE

The End of the Crisis

By the beginning of December 1953, the crisis slowly started to move onto the path of political negotiations between Yugoslavia, Italy and the Allies. Since there were no open hostilities during the crisis, it was much easier to head towards a political solution.[1] Cold autumn days cooled overheated speeches in massive meetings. By late October the Yugoslavs were being conciliatory. In his greetings on 5 November to the 1st Proletarian Division, the main Yugoslav infantry unit deployed in the Trieste vicinity, Tito also introduced a much more moderate approach. After burning statements "You stand on the place where not just our state interests are jeopardized but our land soaked with blood," Tito's conclusion was much more sober "it is [a] burning wish [for] all of us that you should be there ...just as the defender of the peace!"[2]

Ten days later, Tito stated that "Yugoslavia will not go to war because of Trieste, nor will it take Trieste by force."[3] In one other interview, Tito lamented that the notion was created in the worldwide media that the Italians were moderate "and that Yugoslavs want to fight". Tito sent the following message "for many times we said that we are ready to withdraw. But let them withdraw first, since they came first there. Today, I said that we are ready that both armies withdraw and that we solve this question without armies on the borders." Tito explained that "we always have the time to reach where is needed", but insisted on his offer that both armies stood down.[4]

A Yugoslav infantry battalion commander briefs his troops on the military-political situation. (MCO)

A bulletin is distributed to the soldiers in the front line. (MCO)

The first signs of downsizing the alert within the JNA were noted by the beginning of November, when the units in the second line and air bases were returned to "peace-time" working hours and leave for reservists to their homes was also enabled.[5]

Meanwhile, whilst there were the first moderate tones from Tito, the situation in the Trieste became more complicated. Between 4 and 6 November riots raged in the city. There were mass demonstrations in favour of annexation of the city to Italy and Allied military police reacted and clashed with protesters.[6] The riots came to end leaving six dead Italians and dozens of wounded or injured on both sides though Allied forces managed to regain control over the important points in the city.[7]

In Yugoslavia there was a totally different atmosphere: there were elections for the Yugoslav parliament and local communities held on 6 November and the troops headed to the polls with flags and slogans. Warships in the harbours of Zone B were adored with Yugoslav, Communist and naval flags and were surrounded by cheering citizens. The locals in Umag even brought barrels of wine for the sailors.[8]

Although Tito and the political circles in Belgrade were clear that Trieste would never be part of Yugoslavia, their determination and willingness to use force, persuaded Allied governments to abandon the decision to let Italy take control of Zone A by the beginning of December 1953. After that decision of the foreign ministers of the United States, Great Britain and France, on 7 December Italian Prime Minister Pella and Yugoslav ambassador Gregorić signed a document in Rome on the mutual withdrawal of forces from the troubled area of the Free Territory of Trieste. It was decided that all of the surplus forces should be removed back to their garrisons by 20 December.[9]

On 5 December, the Italian General Staff ordered the withdrawal of its units to their regular garrisons and the situation started to normalize. According to the Italian documents, the withdrawal was planned in two phases up to 20 December 1953. Upon the order issued on the 6 December, all of the units were to abandon the border

Yugoslav soldiers voting on the parliamentary elections of 6 November 1953. Italian helmets denote that soldiers belonged to the support branches, most likely communications. (MCO)

Troops packed onto a Dodge lorry, with an inevitable Marshal Tito photograph, heading to the polls in Sezana on 6 November 1953. (MCO)

area, except for the Division *Folgore* and the group belonging to the *Cremona* Division. Those two units started their withdrawal from 12 December. On 8 December, the withdrawal of the Yugoslav forces also started, with a slow return to their normal activities.[10] On the same day at 20:00 hrs the Yugoslav Army cancelled the combat readiness status of its deployed forces. Italian sources noted that one infantry division and all armoured units withdrew from the border line by 13 December. It was agreed upon 20 December that the mass of forces of both armies had been withdrawn from the borders.[11]

Following the order issued on 9 December 1953, the Fifth Military District JNA and its reinforcements were returned to regular daily life. Three days later, on 12 December the *Eskadra* left the ports in Zone B and returned to their regular bases in the mid-Adriatic. It is worth noting that the youngest conscripts had been withdrawn from the units in mid-November and sent back to garrisons to start regular training. Mobilized reservists were sent home, while the oldest conscript contingent from 1951 remained in service for a month more, until their units were withdrawn back to their regular garrisons.[12]

As Colonel Petar Petković, at that time a Mosquito pilot with the 109th Regiment recalls, on the "last day of [the] crisis", crews were summoned by Lt Colonel Ranisavljević, commander of the regiment. He announced to the crowded pilots that an Italian mechanized division had entered Yugoslav territory and was heading for Ljubljana. Ranisavljević ordered that a flight commanded by Captain Franc should take-off and carry out a strike mission. The chosen pilots walked to the prepared Mosquitoes where the regimental security officer provided them with dog-tags. Everything seemed as though "war had started", said Petković. At the runaway the sortie was recalled and surprised crews were radioed to return to their flight-line. This alert was explained as a "motivation check" for the regiment.[13]

Some units remained in the "new" garrisons until the end of the very snowy winter of 1953-54, as was the case with the 83rd Fighter-Bomber Regiment which returned to its parent division in February 1954.[14] The Trieste Crisis was over.

Division of the Free Territory of Trieste

Both adversaries in the Trieste Crisis were backed by the same Allies, and were part of the Mutual Defence Aid Programme. Italy was a member of NATO, while communist Yugoslavia was, besides the MDAP, a member of the Balkan Pact with Greece and Turkey. This Pact was perceived as part of NATO's southern flank. The crisis had separated Yugoslavia from its Balkan Pact allies, Greece and Turkey, which noted at the end of September 1953, that the Yugoslavs cut the flow of military information to both states.[15] The Yugoslavs were cautious that their "military secrets" and other defence related facts and figures would find their way to the belligerent Italy. It was the same case with the United States, which had immediately cancelled the MDAP deliveries. The break lasted between October 1953 and February 1954, when no military item was given to the JNA in the framework of MDAP programme.[16] On 11 March 1954, US President Eisenhower explained to the Yugoslav ambassador in Washington that the United States "have confidence" in Yugoslavia and that the deliveries within the MDAP would be continued. He pointed out that the confidence of the US Congress would be strengthened with Yugoslavia's "generous attitude over Trieste." Eisenhower stressed that they would not cancel the Mutual Assistance Pact with Yugoslavia, but that the solution of the Trieste problem would enable much wider possibilities of cooperation in other fields.[17]

Yugoslav heavy artillery. (MCO)

After six months of negotiations between Yugoslavia on one side and the United States

The Ribnica-based 202nd Artillery Regiment of the Yugoslav Army seen here with 155mm Long Tom guns towed by M5 High-Speed Tractors. (MCO)

The snow-covered ramp at Cerklje air base with Thunderbolts of the 37th Division in the winter of 1953/54. (M. Micevski collection)

and Great Britain on the other, an agreement on a solution of the Trieste question was signed on 31 May 1954. Upon the defined standpoint, FTT was not *de jure* abolished, but was *de facto* separated between Yugoslavia and Italy.[18]

Upon this agreement, Italy received Zone A with the city of Trieste without the minor territory in the Muggia (Milje) peninsula. Yugoslavia received Zone B and the 11.5 square kilometres wide part of Zone A in the Muggia/Milje peninsula with a few villages and hamlets with around 4,000 inhabitants – Slovenes mostly. After Italy signed the treaty, the Allied governments undertook to not support any territorial claims in the area. This would lead to a final solution of the borders between the two states.[19]

Finally, on 5 October 1954, a memorandum of agreement between Italy, Yugoslavia, the United States and Great Britain was signed, meaning that the Trieste question was finally taken off the international negotiating table. According to the agreement signed on 31 May 1954, Yugoslavia and Italy divided the FTT territory upon the agreed lines. The question of

Ground crew of the 172nd FB Regiment posing near their Thunderbolts on 5th December 1953. (A. Smiljanic collection)

Demonstrations in Koper, autumn 1954: "Long Live Annexation of Zone B to Yugoslavia." (MCO)

Removal of the roadblocks on the previous boundary between two zones at the village of Škofije. (MCO)

minorities and traffic were also resolved. This enabled Yugoslavia and Italy to establish firm economic relations in 1955, and launched Italy as the most important economic partner of Yugoslavia for many years.

The Allied forces in the FTT were ordered to abandon Zone A – the city of Trieste. In period between 7 and 14 October 1954, they left the area.[20] British Pathe News reported that 3,000 British troops, including 2nd Battalion Lancashire Fusiliers and the 1st Battalion Loyal (North Lancashire) Regiment were evacuated from the city. "They have been guarding the city for nine years", reported the news and concluded: "The patience and impartiality of the British troops during their stay has contributed greatly to the final peaceful outcome."[21]

TRUST forces began leaving the Free Territory of Trieste in early October 1954. Advance parties moved by military convoy and rail to Livorno. An Italian general met with the TRUST commander at Duino castle to commence planning for the new Italian provisional administration of the main Zone of the FTT. The last British and American troops boarded ships on 26 October 1954 as Italian troops arrived in a heavy rainstorm. The last TRUST commander, Major General John A. Dabney, drove to the airport at Udine, then flew to Livorno to join troops that had already assembled there.[22]

Upon the agreement of General Winterton, the Allied commander in FTT, and Colonel Stamatović, commander of the

A battery of the 320th Artillery Regiment enters Škofije in the former Zone A, on 25 October 1954, armed with Second World War German howitzers Le FH 18 105mm, being towed by MDAP supplied GMC lorries. (MCO)

Italian Ground Forces in North-Eastern Italy 1954[24]

V Army Corps – HQ Padova

Armoured Division *Ariete* – Pordenone
- 132nd Armoured Regiment (I-III Armoured Battalion)
- 8th *Bersaglieri* Regiment (III, V, XII Battalion, AT Coy)
- 132nd Self-Propelled Artillery Regiment
- Light Armoured Squadron *Cavalleggeri Guide*
- CXXXII Engineer Pioneer Battalion
- 132nd Communications Company

Motorised Infantry Division *Folgore* – HQ Treviso
- 182nd Infantry Regiment *Garibaldi*
- 183rd Infantry Regiment *Nembo*
- 5th Light Armoured Regiment *Lancieri di Novara*
- 33rd Artillery Regiment
- 184th Artillery Regiment
- CLXXXIV Engineer Pioneer Battalion
- 184th Communications Company

Infantry Division *Mantova* – HQ Gorizia
- 56th Infantry Regiment *Calabria*
- 76th Infantry Regiment *Napoli*
- 114th Infantry Regiment *Mantova*
- 4th Armoured Cavalry Regiment *Genoa Cavalleri*
- 5th Artillery Regiment
- 155th Artillery Regiment
- CIV Engineer Pioneer Battalion
- 107th Communications Company

Landing Forces Sector – HQ Venezia
- Subsector *Caorle-Grado*
- Subsector *Venezia*
- Subsector *Adige-Po*

Coastal Landing Battalion *Marghera*

Battalion *San Marco* (Navy)

Landing Vehicles Group (Navy)

V Corps units
- 3rd Heavy Artillery Regiment
- 41st Heavy Artillery Regiment
- 5th AD Artillery Regiment – Mestre
- 1st Engineer Pioneer Regiment
- V Communications Battalion
- V Light Aviation Section
- Staff and HQ Units

The Command of the Troops Carnia-Cadore – HQ Belluno

Alpine Brigade *Cadore* – HQ Belluno
- 7th Alpine Regiment (Alpine Battalions *Feltre, Belluno* and *Pieve di Cadore*)
- 6th Mountain Artillery Regiment (four Mt. Art. Groups)
- Engineer Pioneer Company *Cadore*
- Communications Company *Cadore*

Alpine Brigade *Julia* – HQ Cividale del Friuli
- 8th Alpine Regiment (Alpine Battalions *Tolmezzo, Cividale* and L'Aquila)
- 3rd Mountain Artillery Regiment (four Mt. Art. Groups)
- Engineer Pioneer Company *Julia*
- Communications Company *Julia*

Command units:
- XXI Border Group – Paluzza (three border fortification groups)
- XXII Border Group – Gemona (two border fortification groups)
- I, II and III Engineer Pioneer Battalions
- Staff and HQ Units

VI Army Corps – HQ Bologna

Motorised Infantry Division *Trieste* – HQ Bologna
- 40th Infantry Regiment *Bologna*
- 82nd Infantry Regiment *Torino*
- 6th Light Armoured Regiment *Lancieri di Aosta*
- 21st Artillery Regiment
- 121th Artillery Regiment
- VI Engineer Pioneer Battalion
- 6th Communications Company

Infantry Division *Friuli* – HQ Firenze
- 78th Infantry Regiment *Lupi di Toscana*
- 87th Infantry Regiment *Friuli*
- 88th Infantry Regiment *Friuli*
- 2nd Armoured Cavalry Regiment *Piemonte Cavalleria*
- 8th Artillery Regiment
- 35th Artillery Regiment
- CXX Engineer Pioneer Battalion
- 120th Communications Company

VI Corps units:
- VI Tank Battalion,
- II Self-Propelled Artillery Group
- 6th Heavy Artillery Regiment
- 41st Heavy AA Artillery Regiment-Rimini
- 2nd Engineer Pioneer Regiment (I Railway Engineers Bn, II and III Pontoon Engineers Bn),
- VII Corps Communications Battalion
- VI Light Aviation Section
- Recruitment Training Company
- Pontoon Engineer Park Company
- Staff and HQ Units

Other Units:

V Military Territorial Command – Padova
- CXXXIV Security Infantry Battalion
- V Heavy Mortar Group
- Staff and HQ Units

VI Military Territorial Command – Bologna
- 6th Recruitment Training Centre
- 121st Heavy AA Artillery Regiment
- Staff and HQ Units

VII Military Territorial Command – Firenze
- 7th Recruitment Training Centre
- VII Heavy Mortar Group
- 3rd Heavy AA Artillery Regiment – Pisa,
- 7th Engineer Pioneer Company
- Staff and HQ Units
- 3rd Artillery Group for Territory Air Defence – Bologna

Yugoslav Military Government of the FTT, the Yugoslav Army entered the small portion of Zone A that were given to Yugoslavia on 25 October. A few British troops acted as a buffer between the Trieste border police and the Yugoslav forces to prevent any incidents. On the same day Yugoslav civil authorities expanded their responsibilities over Zone B.[23]

On the following day, 26 October, Italian forces spearheaded by the *Bersaglieri* entered the city of Trieste. The honour was a repeat, as the *Bersaglieri* had been the first Italian forces that entered the city on 3 November 1918.[25] The other units which entered the city were of the Infantry Division *Trieste* namely: 82nd Infantry Regiment *Torino* and 1st Group of the 210th Artillery Regiment, and of the Armoured Division *Ariete* (V Battalion of the 8th *Bersaglieri* and 1st Group of Squadrons of the Light Armoured Regiment *Genoa Cavalleria*). The Italian navy arrived and anchored their ships in Trieste harbour: these included the cruiser *Duca degli Abruzzi* and three destroyers *Grecale, Granatiere* and *Artigliere*. The city was overflown by a formation of 24 Thunderjet fighter-bombers from 51st *Aerobrigata*.[26] Crowds cheered enthusiastically for the annexation of the city to the Italian motherland.[27]

Although on a much smaller scale, the same was the case with Slovene inhabitants in Zone B and part of Zone A on the previous day. They cheered the advancing parties of the JNA troops that entered the former Zone A.[28] A month later, on 21 November 1954, Marshal Tito visited the former Zone B. In his speech in Koper, Tito welcomed Slovenes, Croats and Italians from the earlier disputed areas "into new socialist Yugoslavia."[29]

On 26 November 1954 Major General Sir John Winterton left the city for the last time with his

"Greetings hardly expected!" Slovene inhabitants in the part of Zone A annexed by Yugoslavia, welcome the Yugoslav forces 25 October 1954. (MCO)

Yugoslav AA and field artillery at Koper harbour, 25 October 1953. (MCO)

SPECIAL ORDER OF THE DAY

by

Major-General Sir JOHN WINTERTON, KCMG, CB, CBE

GENERAL OFFICER COMMANDING-IN-CHIEF
BRITISH ELEMENT TRIESTE FORCE

On 2 May 1945 TRIESTE was occupied by the 2nd New Zealand Infantry Division and for over nine years units of the British Army have been stationed here, together with the forces of our American Allies. The role of the Army during all this time has been to support the Allied Military Government in the restoration of the normal life of the city and surrounding country and to keep the peace until the future of the Territory could be determined.

Now that this time has arrived and the Allied Troops are being withdrawn from TRIESTE, I feel that we of the British Army can all look back with some pride on what has been achieved.

I congratulate all ranks on the high standard of behaviour which has been shown at all times, and on their tact and dignified bearing. In particular I have admired the spirit with which the special problems of this last year have been faced; the forced separation from wives and families has been loyally and tolerantly borne.

Wherever you may go I wish you all good fortune and hope that you may, once more, be reunited with your families.

On your behalf I wish our American Allies, and our friends in Trieste all success in the future.

TRIESTE
20 OCTOBER 1954

Major General
General Officer Commanding-in-Chief

Intelligence Corps personal security party of Major R M Richards and three sergeants.[30]

After the territories were divided between the two states, an important military downscale started. Yugoslavia disbanded its Military Government of the FTT between December 1954 and mid-1955.[31] The Yugoslav Army Detachment in Zone B (46th Infantry Division) was moved to Novo Mesto and Črnomelj and disbanded there. Its core unit, the 1st Proletarian Infantry Regiment, was moved to Umag and later to Ilirska Bistrica. It had re-joined its parent 1st Proletarian Division which remained the only division level unit in this part of Yugoslavia/Slovenia, with its HQ in Postojna. The 320th Artillery Regiment from Umag was moved to Črnomelj and reorganized into an artillery battalion.[32]

Experiences of Both Armies Gained During the Crisis

The Yugoslav and Italian Army gained many valuable experiences, both positive and negative. One of the crucial experiences for both armies was the relative unexpectedness of the conflict, beside the notion of the dispute which lasted for several years before.

Concerning the Yugoslav Army numerous hardships and problems occurred during the Trieste Crisis especially in the first days of the deployment. It is interesting that the "Operative Report for 1953/54" of the Fifth Military District do not mentioned any of the experiences of the Trieste Crisis, except for mobilisation problems.[33]

Mobilisation was an especially a difficult task for the armoured units since it was very difficult to fulfil the set up time normative for mobilisation (36 hours for a tank brigade). Removal from storage and preparation of the vehicles, preparing live ammunition, and especially charging the enormous number of batteries made the mobilisation of armoured units very difficult.[34]

The accommodation of the troops and organisation of the supply system was one of the most serious problems for the JNA. Due to the massive concentration of the JNA ground forces in the wider area of Trieste, several military schools were moved out from their previous garrisons. The Reserve Infantry Officers School moved from Vipava to Novo Mesto in October 1953.[35] The Military Musical School moved from Trsat near Rijeka to Subotica.[36] The complete air base at Ljubljana (Ljubljana-Polje), consisting of the Higher Aviation Officers School, 465th Air Base and 185th Aviation Regiment, which was exposed to the possibility of immediate Italian attack, was moved to Pula in November 1953.[37]

The Yugoslav Navy and Air Force did not have such problems in the process of mobilisation since their peace-time organisation was almost equal to the one that was planned for war-time. In the Navy there were no reserves – the number of available vessels was identical in peace and war. In the Air Force the differences were only in the number of the airplanes that were out of service, and undergoing repairs and overhaul. The problem for Navy and Air Force was actually the young conscript soldiers who arrived at the units prior to the escalation of the crisis. The problem was evident in the *Eskadra*, which had 50 percent of its conscript sailors belonging to the youngest generation. Their lack of experience produced numerous problems.[38]

Most of the problems for the Yugoslav Navy were logistical. The *Eskadra* arrived in Zone B without information on ammunition and torpedo supplies. The problem was solved much later when delivery was organized from the stores much further south than the area of deployment. The *Eskadra* lacked a fleet workshop which could follow its deployment, while only two small-capacity *peniša* boats were unable to provide fuel in the needed quantities for so many vessels. The feeding of the crews was also solved later, when supplies were taken over by 1st Proletarian Regiment in Koper and 320th Artillery Regiment in Umag.[39]

The organisation of observation and surveillance "suffered" from the lack of skilled observers and communication personnel. It produced a slow flow of information on the appearance of unidentified objects at sea or the activities of the Yugoslav Air Force. The reports reached the *Eskadra* HQ with delays of several hours.

Within the Yugoslav Air Force, the problems were mostly logistical and were related to deliveries of ammunition and bombs from storage. The other problem was the accumulation of aircraft waiting for maintenance and minor repairs since standard procedures were followed, despite the crisis. Another issue was with crews which generally lacked detailed knowledge of the situation and the deployment of the Italian forces. There were examples of ill-discipline, such as delays in sending reports, inadequate paper-work, listening to foreign or music radio stations, and there were some negative comments on the general situation during the crisis among officers or "unhealthy discussions" among reservists "on our armament."[40] Even though the security officers noted such comments, the situation actually was difficult since most of the aircraft really were obsolete (such as Soviet Il-2 and Yak), had inadequate combat capabilities (Ikarus S-49C and even Mosquito) or were even missing such items as radars.

Competing with time, Yugoslav military intelligence

Mobilisation of a JNA reserve unit, 9-10 October 1953. (MCO)

Higgins torpedo-boats of the 76th Squadron, Koper, mid-October 1953. (MCO)

Painted in several different RAF patterns are the Mosquito FB Mk VIs of the 32nd Division, lined-up at Zagreb-Pleso air base. (Author's collection)

Scenes from beginning of the crisis: Yugoslav troops taking positions during the night, against Zone A, in mid-October 1953. (MCO)

(2nd Detachment GS JNA) was forced to change the standard procedures of their intelligence work. The crisis forced them to work on shorter procedures and with improvisations. Although working in a risky fashion, it was remarked that there were no compromises or failure. The Trieste Crisis was rated as the great school for the Yugoslav military intelligence. It started its activities without systematized experience, with modest resources and under complex conditions. The initial work included many mistakes, caused by ignorance and naivety and the Yugoslav Military Intelligence faced on the ground not just Italian military intelligence services but Allied security and intelligence too. They outmatched the Yugoslav intelligence in all matters.

When the Trieste Crisis started the General Staff asked its II Detachment to gather accurate data on Italian conceptions of usage of the armed forces, on its offensive operations, on the usage of the tactical units in all of the branches. Those requests were necessary for other departments of the Yugoslav detachment to organize adequate deployment. "But the Detachment was not able to answer the General Staff request, since it did not possess any kind of such materials except for partial information and examples from other NATO armies." Although the service was "asked much more than it was realistic to expect", it was later estimated that the intelligence service managed to achieve good results, considering its modest knowledge and resources. It was highlighted that Military Intelligence managed to produce daily information which was passed to the Yugoslav military and political leadership. The service regarded them as much more important than those that were "produced" by the civil intelligence services.[41]

The reports of US Army officers on the Yugoslav Army during the crisis, send to Italian General Staff on 15 November 1953, could be accepted as useful commentary on its engagement during the Crisis. The Americans noted the positive and negative sides of JNA. The positive side included: well-trained reservists, good discipline and morale, proper training in driving, leading and manoeuvre with tanks, well-disciplined in camouflage and maintaining communications, good guidance and command as well as orientation and movements. On the negative side, the Americans noted poor tactical knowledge, refusal to use the network of local roads due to their poor quality and maintenance, and little experience and lack of training of all officers, especially those who occupied the command posts at division and higher levels.[42]

General Yugoslav military reports pointed out that the Yugoslav Army carried out important tasks during the Trieste Crisis, and fulfilled the expectations of the state and party leadership as well as the people in the Slovenian Littoral and in the country in general. The determination of the Yugoslav Army not allow any surprises from the Italian side was most likely crucial in further political negotiations between both states and the Allies. Different first-hand experiences were introduced in the regular procedures in the following period.

The Italian armed forces also reported on its engagement in the *"L' esigenza T (Trieste)"*. The whole deployment was with practical experience a huge exercise, but a heavy burden for the whole armed forces. This task gave experience to all components of the Italian armed forces. It effected operations, maintenance, logistics, mobilisation and communication. Almost all of the segments of the Italian armed forces were involved, from General Staff over major HQs to peripheral units including military schools. A total of 294 officers, 525 NCOs and 12,380 soldiers were called to service, while conscripts of the

Although obsolete, Soviet Il-2 Shturmoviks were used in considerable numbers within 37th Division during the crisis. Here is *Gromovnik* (Thunderer) carrying the slogan *Pela – Džukela* (Pela the Mutt). (M. Micevski collection)

generation born in 1931 were kept in their units until the end of the crisis.

The operations were conducted in the near-war conditions with many peace-time limitations. The Italian Army demonstrated efficiency and good proof of discipline and a sprit of sacrifice. The Italians remarked upon the conduct of operations and the large-scale movement of troops to the border area as "regular and on time."

In the domain of the mobilisation of the reservists, Italian estimation said that the flow of the mobilised men reached 90 percent and with later arrival of called-up reservists reached even 100 percent. Italian reports stressed that "nobody rejected the call."

Efficiency and speed in deploying the troops into the area for eventual operations against the Yugoslav forces was especially noted. Transport of the *Cremona* Infantry Division and *Tridentina* Alpine Brigade via railway to the eastern borders was "rapidly organized and carried out". The movement of the *Cremona* Division took a total of 59 hours with 50 trains with a total of 1,750 wagons used. The entire division was moved to a new base in 99 hours from receiving the orders and 82 hours from starting the first train. The movement of the *Tridentina* Brigade was an even greater success, since it had not planned for movement in the case of an emergency and did not have specific organisation predispositions. The movement of the brigade was carried out in 35 hours with total of 21 trains with a total of 650 wagons. The brigade reached the ordered destination in 66 hours from receiving the order and 48 hours from start of the first train.

The Italian side remarked that there were different deficiencies shown in all branches of its armed forces. Peace-time problems resulted in many weaknesses which did not enable instant movement into action of the alerted units. Such experience resulted in the rethinking of the organisational and personnel filling out of the units, as well as in filling out of the outfits with needed equipment, vehicles and organisation of the logistics. The lack of specialist vehicles was evident in the fortification and camouflage works on the ground. The other problems included weak collaboration with the Air Force in organising the eventual close air support, the creation of needed supplies, evident shortages in certain calibres of artillery ammunition, communication equipment and spare parts for vehicles and artillery pieces.[43]

It is most likely that the Trieste Crisis was the most serious military challenge in the long Cold War history of the Yugoslav and Italian armies. After the tragic and difficult experience of the Second World War, the Trieste Crisis actually brought up and demonstrated the successful recovery of Italian morale. In the Yugoslav case, the Trieste Crisis showed the positive morale that was shared by Tito's troops as well as the nation itself. Almost everybody was for war with Italy. The general verve for military action reached its zenith in the history of Cold War Yugoslavia. On the other hand, it provoked problems with NATO allies just at the moment when it was expected that Yugoslavia and its army would strengthen its ties with NATO. Italy gained the benefit from the Yugoslav reaction since it meant that it would not join NATO, and thus Italy lost a potential competitor on the south flank of NATO. Italy and its army remained the sole defender against the communism in that part of Europe.

CONCLUSION

The question of the city of Trieste marked the final stages of the Second World War and beginning of the Cold War in southern Europe in May of 1945: the dispute and open confrontation lasted until the end of the first decade of peace in Europe – until the mid-1950s. Moreover it was the area of confrontation of the two ideologies: western democracy and communism from the east. Even more, in the first after-war years, it was the place where the Iron Curtain was laid between the two worlds and where the Cold War started.

Marshal Tito and the Yugoslav Partisan/Communist-movement-leadership had a clear aim to seize the city during the final stages of the war, while pushing German troops out of the country during the spring of 1945. The importance of the city was twofold, this important and strategic port represented the national aim for the Slovene Communists. In their revolutionary struggle the Yugoslav Partisans combined military force with an immediate political takeover whenever they 'liberated' a certain area or city. But, in the case of Trieste, that policy failed due to the massive Allied troop presence in the city only a day after first Partisan forces had entered. Finally, and in entirely unexpected fashion, Tito's aims lacked support from the USSR and Stalin.

After the June 1945 negotiations a joint military presence was established with limited numbers of Allied and Partisan personnel in the city and neighbouring areas which were divided in two zones, by the so-called Morgan Line. The retreat of the Yugoslav forces from Trieste, did not establish full-scale peace and tranquillity. A temporary solution over the city and wider surrounding area, occasional incidents between the troops and among the civilians of different nationalities, resulted in the Yugoslavs spoiling relations with its former Allies during 1945 and later. Some of those incidents, such as the pointless shooting down of two USAAF cargo planes in the summer of 1946, maintained Yugoslavia's public and media appearance to the Allies as being the villain of the piece. After hard pressure on Tito, Yugoslavia had to remove its air defence aviation assets, no matter that violation of Yugoslav airspace by Allied aircraft continued.

The next stage was the creation of the Free Territory of Trieste in 1947 after the peace treaty with Italy, which redefined the border lines in the area. It included two zones. In Zone A there was the city of Trieste and the surrounding north-west link to the Italian mainland, while Zone B contained small Istrian cities and inland villages populated with Slavs, connected to the Yugoslavian mainland to the south and east. New borders between Italy and Yugoslavia shaped in September 1947, brought another wave of mutual tension, between the Allies and Yugoslavs on the ground.

Yugoslavia broke out from the Informbureau camp in 1948/1949, and from 1951 renewed strong ties with the West through the Military Assistance Pact and programmes of economic aid. The perception of the Trieste question and Italy as a hostile nation did not change, however, despite formidable pressure from the West on Yugoslavia and Tito to realise that the stability of European defence from the Soviets deeply depended on the good relations of all NATO partners including Yugoslavia. Throughout the whole period of Trieste's unresolved status, Yugoslavia maintained a massive military presence in the surrounding area and deeper in to Slovenia and Croatia.

The hard and strict Yugoslav political position, in most cases rooted and backed by populism, had a good counterpart in Italy, which had frequent changes of government, making the new democracy very fragile. The question of Trieste was an excellent issue which could always draw the attention of the nation, pointing to a Communist and Slavic danger, rather than the other questions of the Italian political life. It was the case in September when Italy started to mass its forces with the intention to enter Zone A after the expected Allied decision on dividing the FTT zones between both countries.

The crisis over Trieste culminated in October 1953, when the Allies decided to pass authority over Zone A, which included the city of Trieste itself, to Italy and to withdraw their military contingent. Such a sudden decision provoked one of the most serious Yugoslav military reactions of the Cold War. The sudden military movement towards the Italian border by the Yugoslav troops was fast and sharp. It proved excellent morale and capabilities to fight, which in many cases overcame other problems. Moreover, the crisis of 1953, hampered relations with the NATO allies, just in the same period when the Yugoslavs negotiated for an improved position in the framework of the MDAP and further partnerships.

After the Trieste Crisis reached its end, Western efforts to invite and include Tito's Yugoslavia into NATO's framework slowly vanished, despite the fact that Yugoslavia received armament and equipment through the MDAP for several years further.

All the efforts of the Allies, Yugoslavia and Italy throughout 1954, led to the final solution in the Triesete problem: definitive resolving of the border problems and ending the existence of the Free Territory of Trieste. Negotiations held in London, showed the results of the sometimes contradictory actions: the Allies – wishing to end this problem, and Yugoslavia – with the idea to arrive at a conclusion with minimal cessions to the Italian side. The conflict came to an end when a definitive separation came during October and November 1954. Italy received most of Zone A which included the city of Trieste, while Yugoslavia gained Zone B with minor territorial changes in its favour. The Trieste question and crisis very soon became forgotten, since the economic cooperation between Yugoslavia and Italy started to grow. It remained a page in the history of the earlier stages of the Cold War in Europe.

Bibliography

Archival Sources

ARHIV JUGOSLAVIJE [Archive of Yugoslavia, Belgrade, Serbia]

- fund 112, *TANJUG* [TANJUG-Yugoslav Press Agency]
- fund 130, *Savezno izvršno veće* [Federal Government]
- fund 187, *Savezna uprava za investicije i izgradnju* [Federal Department for Investment and Building]
- fund 837, *Kabinet Predsednika Republike* [Cabinet of the President of Republic]

Diplomatski Arhiv Ministarstva Spoljnih Poslova [Foreign Ministry Diplomatic Archive, Belgrade, Serbia]

- fund PA – *poverljivo* 1945–1954 [Political Archive-Confidential]
- fund PA – *strogo poverljivo* 1945–1954 [Political Archive – Strictly Confidential]

Muzej Jugoslovenskog Ratnog Vazduhoplovstva [Yugoslav Air Force Museum, Belgrade Airport, Serbia]

- fund *jedinice RV i PVO* [Yugoslav Air Force Units]

Public Record Office [Kew, United Kingdom]

- Foreign Office FO 371

Uprava Za Organizaciju, Ministarstvo Odbrane [Department for Organisation, Ministry of Defence, Belgrade, Serbia]

Vojni Arhiv [Military Archive, Belgrade Serbia]

- fund *NOVJ* [People' Liberation Army of Yugoslavia]
- fund *JNA, otvorena i zatvorena građa*, [Yugoslav People's Army – opened and restricted documentation]
- fund *Vojno bezbednosna agencija* [Military Security Agency]

Published sources and official editions

Dokumenti o spoljnoj politici SFRJ, (Savezni sekretarijat za inozemne poslove – Centar za informaciono-dokumentarne poslove Beograd, 1984–1986).

- 1945, volume 2.
- 1946, volumes 1–2.
- 1947, volumes 1–2.
- 1948.

Josip Broz Tito, *Govori i članci* (Naprijed, Zagreb 1959).

- volume 7
- volume 8

Obaveštajna sluzba Sjedinjenih Američkih Država, (DSNO Uprava Bezbednosti, poverljivo, br. evidencije 5921, Beograd 1968).

Razvoj Oružanih snaga SFRJ 1945–1985, (VIZ, Beograd 1986–1991)

- volume 3, *Kopnena vojska* 1-3
- volume 5, *Ratna mornarica*
- volume 13, *Vojnoobaveštajna služba*
- volume 17 *Opremanje naoruzanjem*

Soldier's Guide to the Free Territory of Trieste, (351 Infantry Trieste F.T.T. 1st Edition 4 February 1949).

Titova reč u publikacijama JNA 1941–1980, (VIZ, Beograd 1982).

Zbornik dokumenata i podataka o narodnooslobodilačkom ratu naroda Jugoslavije, volume XI, book 4 (VIZ, Beograd 1975).

XI dalmatinska udarna motostreljačka brigada – Povodom proslave 2. godišnjice osnivanja, (2. oktobar 1945, Skoplje).

Yugoslav military magazines and newspapers

Narodna armija, Front, Narodna Odbrana, Krila armije, Jugoslovenski mornar. Čuvar Jadrana, Za domovinu, Narodni borac, Mornarički glasnik

Yugoslav daily newspapers

Borba, Komunist.

Articles and Chapters in Edited books

Bisenić, Dragan, 'Sveočenje Vladimira Velebita', Politika (Belgrade, 27. mart 2001)

Bogetić, Dragan, 'Odnosi jugoslavije sa zapadom i tršćansko pitanje 1948-1954', *Istorija 20. veka* 1-1994 (Beograd 1994), pp.123-131.

Bogetić, Dragan, 'Iskušenja na putu stvaranja Balkanskog saveza 1952-1955', in collection of works *Balkan posle Drugog svetskog rata* (ISI, Beograd 1996), pp.117-127.

Bogetić, Dragan, 'Londonski pregovori o Trstu i perspektive jugoslovensko-italijanske saradnje', *Jugoslovenski istorijski casopis*, 1-2/2000, (Beograd 2000), pp.169-187.

Bogetić, Dragan, 'Tršćanska kriza i formiranje Balkanskog saveza', *Istorija 20. veka* 1/2001, (Beograd 2001) pp.79-91.

Cappellano, Filippo, 'L' „esigenza T (Trieste)", *Storia militare* n.124 (gennaio 2004), pp.4-24.

Dimitrijević, Bojan, 'The Mutual Defense Aid Program in Tito's Yugoslavia, 1951–1958 and its Technical Impact' (Edited by David M. Glantz), *The Journal of Slavic Military studies* vol. 10, no. 2, June 1997, (London 1997), pp. 19–33.

Dimitrijević, Bojan, 'Jugoslovenska narodna armija u Tršćanskoj krizi 1953. godine', *Istorija 20. veka*, 1/1998, (Beograd 1998), pp. 69–82.

Dimitrijević, Bojan, Petrović, Ognjan, *F-47D Tanderbolt*, Aeroplan 4/1989 (Portoroz 1989).

Dumitrov Dobrivoj, 'Kako je oboren američki avion', *NIN* 16. jun 1985 (Belgrade 1985), p. 8.

Heuser, Beatrice, 'Yugoslavia in Western Military Planing 1948-53', in Marko Milivojević (ed) *Yugoslavia's Security Dilemas*, (Berg, New York 1988), pp.126-136.

Kristen, Samo, 'Ameriški tisk in Trst spomladi 1945 – konec nekega zavenіštva', *Zgodovinski časopis*, leto 1990 1, letnik 44 (Ljubljana 1990).

Malizia, Nicola, 'Testimonianze – Aviano 1953', *Stora militare* n.183. (dicembre 2008), pp.19-27.

Micevski, Milan, and Dimitrijević, Bojan, 'Balkan Mosquitos', *Flypast*, (November 1990) 30-32.

Micevski, Milan, and Dimitrijević Bojan, 'Jakovljev Jak-3', *Aeromagazin*, br. 1, oktobar 1990 (Beograd 1990) pp. 5-25.

Roganović, Mirko, '30 godina jedinica VOJIN', *Glasnik RV i PVO* 3/83 (Beograd 1983).

'Sporazum između vlade FNRJ i vlade SAD o vojnoj pomoći od 14. 11 1951' *Međunarodni ugovori FNRJ* 1/1952, (Belgrade 1952).

Tasić, Dmitar, 'Preoboroževanje enot zagrebško-ljubljanske armadne oblasti s tehniko iz programa zahodne vojaške pomoči v pedesetih letih 20. stoletja', *Vojaška zgodovina*, št.1 (14), vol 9-2008 (Ljubljana 2008) 58-77.

Trifunović, Duško, 'Tukaj smo Slovenci!', *Komunist* 22. jul 1988, (Beograd 1988) 24.

Valdevit, Giampaolo, 'Simetrije i pravila igre, Engleska, Sjedinjene Države i Jugoslavija...', in collection of works *Balkan posle Drugog svetskog rata* (ISI, Beograd 1996), pp.55-69.

Monographs:

Balkanski pakt 1953-1954 – zbornik radova, (VIZ, Beograd 2005).

Bavec, Franjo-Branko, *Na zahodnih mejah 1945. Operativni štab 9. korpusa za zapadno Primorsko* (Društvo piscev zgodovine NOB, Ljubljana 1997).

Bekić, Darko, *Jugoslavija u Hladnom ratu* (Globus, Zagreb 1988).

Biber, Dušan, *Tito–Churchill, Strogo tajno* (Arhiv Jugoslavije Beograd and Globus Zagreb 1981).

Bogetić, Dragan, *Jugoslavija i Zapad 1952-1955* (Sluzbeni list SRJ Beograd 2000).

Bosiočić, Bogdan, *21. slavonska NOU brigada* (VIZ, Beograd 1981).

Bošković, Rajica, *Nebo na dlanu – Vek vazdušnog osmtranja, javljanja i navođenja*, (autorsko izdanje, Beograd 2017).

Cox, Geoffrey, *Road to Trieste* (W. Heinemann, London 1947).

Čerčil S. Vinston, *Drugi svetski rat*, tom 6, *Trijumf i tragedija* (Prosveta, Beograd 1964).

Čuvari našeg neba, (VIZ, Beograd 1977).
Dimitrijević, Bojan i MICEVSKI Milan, 9999*JETS, avioni američkog porekla u jugoslovenskom naoružanju 1953–1974* (Spektar, Beograd 1991).
Dimitrijević, Bojan, *Od Staljina do Atlantskog pakta, Armija u spoljnoj politici Titove Jugoslavije 1945-1958* (Sluzbeni list SRJ, Beograd 2005).
Dimitrijević, Bojan, *Jugoslovensko ratno vazduhoplovstvo 1942–1992* (ISI, Beograd 2006).
Dimitrijević, Bojan, and Bogetić, Dragan, *Tršćanska kriza 1945-1954, vojno-politički aspekti* (ISI, Beograd 2009).
Dimitrijević, Bojan, *Jugoslovenska narodna armija 1945–1959* (ISI, Beograd 2014).
Dimitrijević, Bojan, *Bitka za Trst 1945-1954* (Despot Infinitus, Zargeb 2014).
Dimitrijević, Bojan and Micevski, Milan, *117. lovački puk*, (Galaksija. Niš 2015).
Đilas, Milovan, *Druženje s Titom* (Izdavači Milovan Đilas i Momčilo Đorgović, Beograd 1990).
Đurić, Ljuban, *7. banijska brigada Vasilj Gaćeša* (VIZ, Beograd 1981).
Enciklopedija Jugoslavije, knjiga 8 (Jugoslovenski leksikografski zavod, Zagreb 1971).
Finansijska služba JNA, Nastanak u NOR-u i razvoj do 1985 (VIZ, Beograd 1988).
1. dalmatinska proleterska brigada (VIZ, Beograd 1986).
Di Giusto, Stefano, *Operationszone Adriatisches Küstenland* (Instituto Furlano per la Storia del Movimento Liberazoone, Udine 2005).
Italian Air force, 1945–1978 (Military Air Arms series, Midland Co. publ. 1983).
Jakšić Pavle, *Nad uspomenama*, drugi deo (Rad, Beograd 1990).
Jović, Stojan, *Pod kupolom padobrana*, (Narodna armija Beograd 1980).
Lah Borivoj-Boris, *Štirikrat čez Sočo, Osvobodilni boj primorskega ljudstva v brigadi Simona Gregorčiča* (Društvo Piscev Zgodovine NOB Slovenije, Ljubljana 1998).
Lazić Branko, *Titov pokret i režim u Jugoslaviji 1941–1946* (NIP Dečje novine, Gornji Milanovac 1992).
Lees M., Lorraine, *Keepin Tito Afloat, The United States, Yugoslavia and the Cold* War, (Penn State University Press, 2003).
Ličina, Đuro, *Tragom plave lisice* (CID, Zagreb 1990).
Likso, Tihomir, *Letačka karijera Miljenka Lipovšćaka 1939–1980* (D. Canak Nova Gradiška 2000).
Lindsay, Franklin, *Beacons in the Night with the OSS and Tito's Partisans in War-time Yugoslavia* (Stanford University Press California 1993).
Micevski, Milan and Dimitrijević, Bojan, *83. lovački puk* (Galaksijanis, Niš 2016).
Milkić, Miljan, *Tršćanska kriza u vojnopolitičkim odnosima Jugoslavije sa velikim silama 1943-1947* (INIS, Beograd 2012).
Mikolić, Mario, *Istra 1941-1947,Godine velikih preoreta* (BARBAT, Zagreb 2003).
Novak C. Bogdan, *Trieste 1941–1954, The Ethnic, Political and Ideological Struggle* (University of Chicago Press 1970).
Od osvobodilnega boja do banditizma, Pričevanje nekdanjga Mačekovega pomoćnika Alberta Svetine (Nova obzorja, Ljubljana 2011).
Pejčić, Predrag, *Tito među vazduhoplovcima*, (VIZ, Beograd 1979).
Pejčić, Predrag, *Čelična krila*, (Eskportpress, Beograd 1985).
Petković, Ranko, *Jedan vek odnosa Jugoslavije i SAD* (VINC Beograd 1992).
Rabel G, Roberto, *Between East and West, Trieste, the United States and the Cold War 1941-1954*, (Duke University Press, Durham and London 1988).
Radica, Bogdan, *Hrvatska 1945*, (Knjiznica Hrvatske Revije, Minhen–Barcelona 1974).
Ridli, Džasper, *Tito, biografija*, (Buducnost, Novi Sad 1998).
Sinobad, Milos, *103. izvidjacki avijacijski puk*, (Milos Sinobad, Beograd 2008).
Šalov, Mate, *3. dalmatinska brigada*, (Institut za historiju radničkog pokreta Dalmacije, Split 1988).
Vidmar, Cvetko, *Zadnja tuja vojaška okuapcija slovenskega ozemlja, Oris zavezniške vojaške uprave v Slovenskem primorju od 12. junija 1945 do 15. septembra* (Goriški muzej, Nova Gorica 2009).
Westlake, Ray, *English and Welsh Infantry Regiments, An Illustrated Record of Service 1662-1994*, (Spellmount, Staplehurst, 2002).
Zapisi i komentari, O školovanju i životu II klase Vojnopomorske akademija Jugoslovenske ratne mornarice (Beograd 2008).

Notes

Chapter 1

1 *Zbornik dokumenata i podataka o narodnooslobodilačkom ratu naroda Jugoslavije*, vol. XI, book 4, (VIZ, Beograd 1975), p. 890.
2 di Giusto, Stefano, *Operationszone Adriatisches Küstenland*, (Instituto Furlano per la Storia del Movimento Liberazone, Udine 2005), pp. 658-666; *Zbornik dokumenata* XI, 4, pp. 344-349; Mikolić, Mario, *Istra 1941-1947, godine velikih preokreta*, (BARBAT Zagreb 2003), pp. 356-367.
3 *Zbornik dokumenata* XI, 4, p. 454.
4 Novak C. Bogdan, *Trieste 1941–1954, The Ethnic, Political and Ideological Struggle* (University of Chicago Press 1970), p. 156.
5 *Zbornik dokumenata* XI, 4, p. 667.
6 di Giusto, *Operationszone Adriatisches Küstenland*, pp. 684-685.
7 *Zbornik dokumenata* XI, 4, p. 501; di Giusto, *Operationszone Adriatisches Küstenland*, pp. 684-685.
8 *Zbornik dokumenata* XI, 4, pp. 502, 838-839, 840-842, 871, 873; Lah-Boris, Borivoj, *Štirikrat čez Sočo, Osvobodilni boj primorskega ljudstva v brigadi Simona Gregorčiča*, (Društvo Piscev Zgodovine NOB Slovenije Ljubljana 1998), p. 203.
9 *Zbornik dokumenata* XI, 4, pp. 622, 716-720.
10 Novak, *Trieste 1941–1954*, pp. 161-162, 165; Vojni arhiv (VA): fund NOB: k. 312, 1/1, 36/1; *Zbornik, Zbornik dokumenata* XI, 4, pp. 841, 856–893.
11 Lazić, Branko, *Titov pokret i režim u Jugoslaviji 1941–1946*, (NIP Dečje novine, Gornji Milanovac 1992), pp. 184–185.
12 Geoffrey, Cox, *Road to Trieste*, (W. Heinemann, London 1947), pp. 1–7, 192, 200–210; Novak, *Trieste 1941–1954*, p. 163.
13 *Zbornik dokumenata* XI, 4, p, 1069.
14 BETFOR Association, *The Liberation of Trieste by the 9th Brigade of the New Zealand Division, part of the British Eighth Army in Italy*. <http:// betforassociation.org /Betforliberation.html> (accessed 26 August 2018).
15 *Zbornik dokumenata* XI, 4, p, 1038; Valdevit Giampaolo, 'Simetrije i pravila igre, Engleska, Sjedinjene Države i Jugoslavija…', in collection of works *Balkan posle Drugog svetskog rata* (ISI, Beograd 1996), p. 60.
16 Lindsay, *Beacons in the Night With the OSS*, p. 304-306; Milkić Miljan, *Tršćanska kriza u vojnopolitičkim odnosima Jugoslavije sa velikim silama 1943-1947* (INIS, Beograd 2012), pp.88-90.
17 Bavec-Branko, Franjo, *Na zahodnih mejah 1945, Operativni štab 9. korpusa za zapadno Primorsko,* (Društvo piscev zgodovine NOB, Ljubljana 1997), pp. 377-380.
18 Valdevit, 'Simetrije i pravila igre', p. 60.
19 Čerčil S. Vinston, *Drugi svetski rat*, tom 6, *Trijumf i tragedija*, (Prosveta, Beograd 1964), p.499.
20 Cox, *Road to Trieste*, pp.227-228; Novak, *Trieste 1941–1954*, pp. 181, 183.
21 VA: JNA-zatvorena građa: svž. 678, f.41 (2.tbr); *XI dalmatinska udarna motostreljačka brigada – Povodom proslave 2. godišnjice osnivanja*, (2. oktobar 1945 Skoplje), pp. 35-39.
22 Čerčil, *n. d.*, p. 501.
23 *Razvoj Oružanih snaga SFRJ 1945–1985*, vol. 13 'Obaveštajna služba' (VIZ Beograd 1991), p. 252.
24 Rabel G, Roberto, *Between East and West, Trieste, the United States and the Cold War 1941-1954*, Duke University Press, Durham and London 1988. p. 72.
25 Lindsay A Franklin, *Beacons in the Night With the OSS and Tito's Partisans in War-time Yugoslavia*, (Stanford University Press, California 1993), p. 291.
26 Lindsay, *Beacons in the Night With the OSS*, p. 307
27 *Soldier's Guide to the Free Territory of Trieste*, (351 Infantry Trieste F.T.T. 1st Edition 4 February 1949), pp. 24-25; Novak, *Trieste 1941–1954*, pp. 199.
28 *Dokumenti o spoljnoj politici SFRJ*, 1945 vol. 2 (Savezni sekretarijat za inozemne poslove – Centar za informaciono-dokumentarne poslove Beograd, 1985), p. 81; Novak, *Trieste 1941–1954*, pp. 199–200; *Zbornik dokumenata* XI, 4, pp. 1100–1101.
29 VA: NOB: k. 1029/II, 6,7; VA: NOB: k 1030, f-2.
30 BETFOR Association, *The Intelligence Corps in Venezia Giulia 1945 – 1954*, <http://betforassociation.org/
BETFORTSO.html>, (accessed on 26 August 2018).
31 *Zbornik dokumenata* XI, 4, p. 892.
32 VA: JNA: svž. 678, f. 40 (1.tbr).
33 *Zbornik dokumenata* XI, 4, p. 892; *1. dalmatinska proleterska brigada* (VIZ, Beograd 1986), p. 432; Šalov, Mate, *3. dalmatinska brigada*, (Institut za historiju radničkog pokreta Dalmacije, Split 1988), pp. 497–498. Bavec, *Na zahodnih mejah 1945*, pp. 383-386; Mikolić, *Istra 1941-1947*, p. 371; Vidmar, Cvetko, *Zadnja tuja vojaška okuapcija slovenskega ozemlja, Oris zavezniške vojaške uprave v Slovenskem primorju od 12. junija 1945 do 15. septembra* (Goriški

muzej, Nova Gorica 2009), p. 235.

34 Valdevit, 'Simetrije i pravila igre', p. 69; *Soldier's Guide to the Free Territory of Trieste*, p. 25.

35 *Soldier's Guide to the Free Territory of Trieste*, p. 25.

36 *Zbornik dokumenata* XI, 4, pp. 1100–1101.

37 Mikolić, *Istra 1941-1947*, p. 372.

38 *Od osvobodilnega boja do banditizma, Pričevanje nekdanjga Mačekovega pomoćnika Alberta Svetine,* (Nova obzorja, Ljubljana 2011), pp. 185-188, 214-215; Radica Bogdan, *Hrvatska 1945*, (Knjiznica Hrvatske Revije, Minhen–Barcelona 1974), pp. 193-194, 202; Novak, *Trieste 1941–1954,* pp. 179–180.

39 VA: NOB: k. 25a 8/2, 2143/1; Milkić, *Tršćanska kriza u vojnopolitičkim odnosima Jugoslavije*, pp. 103-106.

40 *Dokumenti 1945*, pp. 82, 98–102; *Zbornik dokumenata* XI, 4, p. 1102.

41 Bavec, *Na zahodnih mejah 1945,* pp. 384; Ljuban Đurić, 7. banijska brigada Vasilj Gaćeša, (VIZ, Beograd 1981), pp. 371–372; Vidmar, *Zadnja tuja vojaška okuapcija slovenskega ozemlja*, p. 235-236.

42 Vidmar, *Zadnja tuja vojaška okuapcija slovenskega ozemlja*, p. 239.

43 *Razvoj OS SFRJ*, vol. 13, pp. 256-258.

44 Novak, *Trieste 1941–1954,* p. 234.

45 *Dokumenti 1945*, p. 112; Novak, *Trieste 1941–1954,* pp. 234.

46 *Od osvobodilnega boja do banditizma*, pp. 214, 220-248.

47 Novak, *Trieste 1941–1954,* p. 203.

48 Vidmar, *Zadnja tuja vojaška okuapcija slovenskega ozemlja*, pp. 99, 105, 240-241.

49 BETFOR *Orbat,* <http://betforassociation.org/betfororbat.html> (accssesed 26 August 2018); Westlake, Ray, *English and Welsh Infantry Regiments, An Illustrated Record of Service 1662-1994*, (Spellmount, Staplehurst, 2002).

50 BETFOR, *The Intelligence Corps in Venezia Giulia 1945 - 1954*, <http://betforassociation.org/BETFORTSO.html> (accessed 26 August 2018).

51 *Dokumenti o spoljnoj politici Jugoslavije,* 1946, vol I (Savezni sekretarijat za inozemne poslove - Centar za informaciono-dokumentarne poslove Beograd, 1985), p. 37.

52 *Dokumenti 1946,* vol I, pp. 84, 85; *Narodna armija*, 12 March 1946.

53 VA: JNA: svž. 678, f.41 (2.tbr); VA: JNA: svž. 603, 'Operativni izveštaj o dislokaciji i detašovanju jedinica broj 4, Štab I tbr, Vrhnika 14-II-1946'.

54 Bosiočić Bogdan, *21. slavonska NOU brigada*, (VIZ, Beograd 1981), p. 323.

55 Memorial Room of the 111th Aviation Brigade, Zagreb-Pleso Air Base, *Istorijat 422./111. jurišnog puka za 1946. godinu* (author visited this facility on 20th July 1987); Muzej Jugoslovenskog ratnog vazduhoplovstva (MJRV): fund RV i PVO: k. 30, *Istorijat 116. lovačkog puka*, 5.

56 Diplomatski arhiv Ministarstva spoljnih poslova (DAMSP): Poverljiva arhiva (PA): 1946, f-47, 7, 10144.

57 DAMSP: PA: 1946, f-3, 7, 2047; isto, f-3, 7, 2357; isto, f-3, 8, 5103.

58 DAMSP: PA: 1946, f-47, 7, 10144; *Dokumenti 1946-I*, 84, 85, 89, 177-178, 278, 280; *Narodna armija,* 22. jun 1946.

59 MJRV: fund RV i PVO: 3-1/1, *Istorija 3 vazduhoplovne lovacke divizije u 1946. godini*; DAMSP, PA, 1946, f-47, 6, 9767; DAMSP, PA, f-47, 6, 9958; DAMSP, PA, f-47, 7, 9860. *Dokumenti o spoljnoj politici SFRJ*, 1946, vol. 2, (Savezni sekretarijat za inozemne poslove - Centar za informaciono-dokumentarne poslove Beograd, 1985) 14; Dumitrov, Dobrivoj, 'Kako je oboren američki avion', *NIN*, (Belgrade, 16. jun 1985), 8.

60 MJRV: RV i PVO: 3-1/1; DAMSP: PA: 1946, f-47, 6, 9958; Dumitrov, *Kako je oboren američki avion*; Authors' interview with ret. Col. Dobrivoje Dumitrov Belgrade September 1986.

61 DAMSP: PA: 1946, f-3, 8, 186; Ridli, Džasper, *Tito, biografija*, (Buducnost, Novi Sad 1998), p. 251.

62 DAMSP: PA: 1946, f-47, 7, XLIII-126, 153; DAMSP: PA: f-47, 7, 10310, 10440 and 11715; DAMSP: PA: 1947, f-59, 15, 10658 and 11593.

63 DAMSP: PA: 1946, f-47, 7, 10310 – for details on further violations of Yugoslav air space and territorial waters in 1946, see the daily reports of the Yugoslav General Staff, YAF HQs and KNOJ HQs in: DAMSP: PA: 1946, f-47, 9–16. For 1947 see: DAMSP: PA: 1947, f-59, and for 1948 see: DAMSP: PA: 1948, f-86.

64 *Borba,* 15th September 1946; *Dokumenti* 1946, vol I, 205; *Dokumenti* 1946, vol II, 127; *Dokumenti o spoljnoj politici SFRJ,* 1947-I, (Savezni sekretarijat za inozemne poslove - Centar za informaciono-dokumentarne poslove Beograd, 1986), pp. 113–115, 122–124.

Chapter 2

1 *Enciklopedija Jugoslavije,* knjiga 8 (Jugoslovenski leksikografski zavod, Zagreb 1971), pp 377; Vidmar, *Zadnja tuja vojaška okuapcija slovenskega ozemlja*, p. 317.

2 *Soldier's Guide to the Free Territory of Trieste*, p. 25.

3 *Dokumenti o spoljnoj politici SFRJ,* 1947, vol. II (Savezni sekretarijat za inozemne poslove - Centar za informaciono-dokumentarne poslove Beograd, 1986), p. 165; Vidmar, *Zadnja tuja vojaška okuapcija slovenskega ozemlja*, p. 321.

4 *Soldier's Guide to the Free Territory of Trieste*, pp. 25-33.

5 *Dokumenti o spoljnoj politici SFRJ,* 1947, vol. II, p. 165; Vidmar, *Zadnja tuja vojaška okuapcija slovenskega ozemlja*, p. 321.

6 *Razvoj OS SFRJ*, vol. 13, 254; Vujić Trivo, *Knjiga sećanja*, (Nepoznati izdavač, Beograd 1980), p. 276.

7 Vujić, *Knjiga sećanja* , pp. 266, 267, 272.

8 VA: JNA: svž. 2278 d. 2, 'Naredba IV armije st.pov 333 od 18. marta 1947'. VA: JNA: svž. 603, 'Dnevnik 1. tbr za 1947'; VA: JNA:, svž. 604, 'Operacijski dnevnik Motomehanizovanog puka, broj 1 za 1947.g'.

9 VA: JNA: svž. 603 'Dnevnik I tbr za 1947'.

10 Vidmar, *Zadnja tuja vojaška okuapcija slovenskega ozemlja*, pp. 321-322.

11 Vidmar, *Zadnja tuja vojaška okuapcija slovenskega ozemlja*, pp. 322-323.

12 'Sa Jugoslovenskom armijom od Tolmina do Predilskog prelaza' *Front*, 55, 1st October 1947.

13 MJRV: RV i PVO: 3-2/1, *Istorija 3 vazduhoplovne lovacke divizije, od 1.4.47 do 1.4.48*. Further details in: Dimitrijevic, Bojan and Micevski, Milan, *117. lovacki puk*, (Galaksija Nis 2015), and Micevski, Milan and Dimitrijevic, Bojan, *83. lovacki puk* (Galaksijanis Nis 2016).

14 Vidmar, *Zadnja tuja vojaška okuapcija slovenskega ozemlja*, p. 324.

15 Lindsay, *Beacons in the Night*, pp. 330-331.

16 Vidmar, *Zadnja tuja vojaška okuapcija slovenskega ozemlja*, p. 322.

17 *Soldier's Guide to the Free Territory of Trieste*, p. 13.

18 *Razvoj OS SFRJ,* vol 5, 'Ratna mornarica', (VIZ, Beograd 1988), p. 43.

19 MJRV: RV i PVO: 3-2/1; Interview with ret. General Mihajlo-Kajle Nikolić with Milan Micevski and the author, Zemun, September 1990.

20 Novak, *Trieste 1941–1954,* p. 322, 330.

21 *Finansijska služba JNA, Nastanak u NOR-u i razvoj do 1985,* (VIZ Beograd 1988), p. 58.

22 Arhiv Jugoslavije (AJ): fund 187 'Savezna uprava za investicije i izgradnju': 2-10.

23 Uprava za organizaciju, Ministarstvo odbrane Republike Srbije (UO-MoD): III uprava GŠ JA, 'Knjiga mobilizacijskog razvoja JA i KNOJ-a prema naređenju 67 od 24. jula 1949.'

24 UO-MoD: Naredba DSNO pov. br. 830/52 'kao dopuna knjige mobilizacijskog razvoja JA i KNOJ-a prema naređenju 67 od 24. jula 1949.'

25 VA: JNA: k.13, f.1, d.1 / map; UO-MoD: III uprava GŠ JA, 'Knjiga mobilizacijskog razvoja JA i KNOJ-a prema naređenju 67 od 24. jula 1949.'

26 UO-MoD: III uprava GŠ JA, 'Knjiga mobilizacijskog razvoja JA i KNOJ-a prema naređenju 67 od 24. jula 1949.'

27 *Soldier's Guide to the Free Territory of Trieste*, pp. 13-15.

28 *Directory and Station Lists, Trieste United States Troops, Published by The Adjutant General's Office, Washington D.C.*13 June 1952, <https://www.usarmygermany.com/Sont.htm?https&&&www.usarmygermany.com/Units/TRUST/TRUST_main.htm> (accessed 26 August 2018).

29 *Directory and Station Lists, Trieste United States Troops,* 16 August 1954, <https://www.usarmygermany.com/Sont.htm?https&&&www.usarmygermany.com/Units/TRUST/TRUST_main.htm> (accessed 26 August 2018).

30 *Commanding Generals, Trieste United States Troops*, <https://www.usarmygermany.com /Sont.htm?https&&&www.usarmygermany.com/Units/TRUST/TRUST _main.htm> (accessed 26 August 2018).

31 BETFOR, *Orbat* <http://betforassociation.org/betfororbat.html> (accsses 26 August 2018); Westlake, *English and Welsh Infantry Regiments.*

32 *Soldier's Guide to the Free Territory of Trieste*, pp. 50-52.

33 *Soldier's Guide to the Free Territory of Trieste*, pp. 50-52.

34 BETFOR, *The Intelligence Corps in Venezia Giulia 1945 - 1954*, <http://betforassociation.org/BETFORTSO.html> (accessed on 26 August 2018).

35 L'Esercito Italiano nel 1949< http://nuovadifesa.altervista.org/lesercito-italiano-nel-1949/ > (accessed on 11 September 2018).

36 *Dokumenti o spoljnoj politici SFRJ,* 1948, (Savezni sekretarijat za inozemne poslove - Centar za informaciono-dokumentarne poslove Beograd, 1986Beograd 1986), pp. 25–26, 30–33, 82–84, 107–108, 143, 149–150.

37 *Narodna odbrana,* 48, (Beograd 1949), p. 5.

38 Cappellano Filippo, 'L' „esigenza T (Trieste)", *Storia militare* n.124 (gennaio 2004), p. 6.

39 BETFOR, *The Intelligence Corps in Venezia Giulia 1945 - 1954.*

40 Rabel G, Roberto, *Between East and West, Trieste, the United States and the Cold War 1941-1954*, Duke University Press, Durham and London 1988. Preface, XI.

41 For political context and details see: Lees M. Lorraine, *Keepin Tito Afloat, The United State, Yugoslavia and the Cold* War, (Penn State University Press, 2003); Heuser, Beatrice, 'Yugoslavia in Western Military Planning 1948-53', in Marko Milivojević (ed) *Yugoslavia's Security Dilemas*, (Berg, New York 1988), 126-136.

42 Bisenić Dragan, 'Sveočenje Vladimira Velebita', *Politika* (Belgrade, 27, 31 March and 3 April 2001); VA: JNA: k. 14, f.7; DAMSP: PA: str. pov f-11, 2, 1653, *zabeleška* 1-7; Bekić Darko, *Jugoslavija u Hladnom ratu* (Globus, Zagreb 1988), pp.232-233, 280-282, 286-287.

43 *Borba*, (Belgrade 15-16.oktobar 1951); DAMSP: PA: str. pov, 1951, f-9, 7, 1687; *Razvoj OS SFRJ 1945-1985*, volume 3-2 'Kopnena vojska' (VIZ, Beograd 1988), p. 171; 111th Aviation Brigade, Zagreb-Pleso Air Base, *Istorijat 111. avijacijskog puka za 1951. godinu.*

44 VA: fond JNA: k. 14, f.9, 2/1; DAMSP, PA, str. pov, 1951, f-9, 7, 1902 and 2176; DAMSP, PA str.pov 1952, f-75, 21, 417486; *Borba* (Belgrade, 15 Novembar 1951 and 13 Februar 1952), 1-3; *Obavestajna sluzba Sjedinjenih Američkih Država,* (DSNO, Uprava Bezbednosti, poverljivo, br. evidencije 5921, Beograd 1968), p. 47; "Sporazum između vlade FNRJ i vlade SAD o vojnoj pomoći od 14. 11 1951" *Međunarodni ugovori FNRJ* 1/1952, (Belgrade 1952); Petković Ranko, *Jedan vek odnosa Jugoslavije i SAD* (VINC Beograd 1992), pp. 102-105.

45 Tito, Josip Broz , *Govori i članci* , vol. VII (Naprijed, Zagreb 1959), pp. 13 and 195.

46 MJRV: RV i PVO: *Registri aviona Komande JRV i 7.vazduholpvnog korpusa za 1951-1952,* MJRV: RV i PVO: *Dokumentacija komisije za prijem tehnike iz okvira zapadne vojne pomoći, za tip Moskito*; Micevski, Milan and Dimitrijevic, Bojan, 'Balkan Mosquitos', *Flypast*, (November 1990) 30-32.

47 Pejčić Predrag, *Tito među vazduhoplovcima*, (VIZ, Beograd 1979); Dimitrijević Bojan, Petrović Ognjan, *F-47D Tanderbolt*, Aeroplan 4/1989 (Portoroz 1989).
48 *Razvoj OS SFRJ*, vol 3-2, chapters on armoured units and artilery. *Balkanski pakt 1953-1954 - zbornik radova, (VIZ, Beograd 2005) pp. 377-387; Tasić Dmitar, 'Preoboroževanje enot zagrebško-ljubljanske armadne oblasti s tehniko iz programa zahodne vojaške pomoči v pedesetih letih 20. stoletja', Vojaška zgodovina*, št.1 (14), vol 9-2008 (Ljubljana 2008) 58-77.
49 VA: fund VBA: k.10, 6.3.02, sv. 25. 63-78.
50 VA: JNA: k.19, f.1, 4/32 'Prijem nove tehnike u periodu od 1 XI 1952 do 20 VIII 1953'.
51 VA: JNA: k.19, f.1, 4/1; UO-MoD: 'Naredba DSNO pov. br. 830/52.'; *Razvoj OS SFRJ*, vol.17 'Opremanje naoruzanjem' (VIZ Beograd 1989) pp. 174-176.
52 VA: JNA: k.19, f.1, 4/1.
53 VA: JNA: k.21, f.3. 3,14.
54 Novak, *Trieste 1941–1954*, p. 363.
55 Novak, *Trieste 1941–1954*, p. 320.
56 Dimitrijević Bojan, Bogetić Dragan, *Tršćanska kriza 1945-1954, vojno-politički aspekti* (ISI, Beograd 2009), p. 43.
57 DAMSP: PA: 1952, str.pov. f-4, , 974; Bekić, *Jugoslavija u Hladnom ratu*, pp. 375-377.
58 DAMSP: PA: 1952, str.pov, f-15, 1007.
59 AJ: fund 837 Kabinet Predsednika Republike: KPR I, 2/1 'Stenografske zabeleške sa zvaničnih razgovora prilikom posete Druga Predsednika Londonu (16–21. marta 1953)'.
65 Novak, *Trieste 1941–1954*, p. 237.

Chapter 3

1 Dimitrijević - Bogetić, Tršćanska kriza, pp. 66-67.
2 DAMSP: PA: 1953, SAD, f-80, 412 344.
3 DAMSP: PA: 1953, SAD, f-22, 417 319.
4 DAMSP: PA: 1953, SAD, f-79, 412 124.
5 DAMSP: PA: 1953, f-41, 2, 4,5; *Borba*, (Belgrade, 5 and 16 January, 14 February, 6 March, 4 April 1953); *Čuvar Jadrana*, 223, (Split 5 December 1952).
6 AJ: fund 112 Tanjug: 1062/1063, *Specijalni informativni bilten*, 1 September 1953.
7 *Borba*, (Belgrade, 11, 22 June, 27 July 1953).
8 AJ: fund 112 Tanjug: 1062/1063, *Specijalni informativni bilten*, 1 September 1953.
9 *Borba*, (Belgrade, 19, 27, 31 August, 1–5 September 1953).
10 UO-MoD: Naredba DSNO pov. br. 830/52 'kao dopuna knjige mobilizacijskog razvoja JA i KNOJ-a prema naređenju 67 od 24. jula 1949' and author's further research.
11 Bekić, *Jugoslavija u Hladnom ratu*, pp. 535–536; Novak, *Trieste 1941–1954*, p. 421.
12 Cappellano, *L' „esigenza T (Trieste)"*.
13 The HQ of the V Corps (V Corpo) was reformed on 1 May 1952 in Padova. On the 30 September 1953 this HQ moved to Vittorio Veneto in Palazzo Piccin with the task to ensure the defence on the north-eastern borders. Corps maintained three divisions, Armoured Division *Ariete* at Pordenone, Motorised Infantry Division *Folgore* at Treviso and Infantry Division *Mantova* with has the HQs in Gorizia. *V Corpo d'armata (Esercito Italiano)* at <https://it.wikipedia.org/wiki/V_Corpo_d%27armata_(Esercito_Italiano)> (Accessed 26 August 2018).
14 Malizia Nicola, 'Testimonianze – Aviano 1953', *Stora militare* n.183. (dicembre 2008), pp. 24-25.
15 Cappellano, *L' „esigenza T (Trieste)"*, p.14.
16 Malizia, *Testimonianze – Aviano 1953*, pp. 24-25.
17 *Italian Air force, 1945–1978* (Military Air Arms series, Midland Co. publ. 1983). pp 55, 56, 61; Cappellano, *L' „esigenza T (Trieste)"*, p. 12.
18 VA: fond JNA: 5384/1977, *Pregled operativnog bojnog stanja posada iaviona sa resursima JRV u 1953. godini*, table: 1 October 1953.
19 *Razvoj OS SFRJ*, vol. 5 'Ratna mornarica', Beograd 1988, pp. 55, 60.
20 Dedicated forces were Tactical Group T consisting of the *Genoa* Regiment and two battalions of Bersaglieri, Tactical Group M consisted of battalions *San Marco* and *Marghera* and a mortar company which arrived on ships; and a paratrooper unit which was intended to carry out airborne landing in Zone A. A reserve was created around a group from the *Novara* light armoured regiment with M-26 Pershing tanks. It was ordered that the first unit to enter the Trieste would be a company of the 12th Battalion of *Bersaglieri* and the regimental band.
21 Cappellano, *L' „esigenza T (Trieste)"*.
22 *Narodna armija*, 737 (Belgrade 3 September 1953), pp. 1, 5.
23 *Borba* (Belgrade, 5, 6. i 7. septembar 1953).
24 Tito, Josip Broz, *Govori i članci* vol. VIII, (Naprijed, Zagreb 1959), pp 198–201.
25 Bekić, *Jugoslavija u Hladnom ratu*, p. 535.
26 DAMSP, 1953, f-41, 2; *Narodna armija*, 738 (Belgrade 10. septembar 1953).
27 Tito, *Govori i članci* vol. VIII, pp. 209–214.
28 *Razvoj OS SFRJ*, vol. 5, p. 50 and appendix 7.
29 *Razvoj OS SFRJ*, vol. 5, pp. 48–49.
30 Novak, *Trieste 1941–1954*, p. 162.
31 *Razvoj OS SFRJ*, vol. 5, pp. 49–50.
32 Cappellano, *L' „esigenza T (Trieste)"*, p. 18.
33 DAMSP, 1953, f-41, 2; *Borba* (Beograde 5, 6, 7, 10, 12, 13,15 and 26 September 1953).
34 Malizia, *Testimonianze – Aviano 1953*, 25-26. Also, further research of Milan Micevski, interview with Jaksic's relatives in Belgrade February 2018.
35 *Borba* (Belgrade 22, 30 September, 1, 9 October 1953).
36 *Narodna armija*, 735, (Belgrade, 20 August 1953); *Za domovinu*, 19, (Zagreb 20 August 1953); *Borba*, (Belgrade 15 August 1953).
37 MJRV: RV i PVO: 'Operacijski dnevnik 32. lbad/14. mad, za period avgust–novembar 1953'; *Razvoj OS SFRJ*, vol. 5, pp. 48–49.
38 *Za domovinu*, (Zagreb, 20, 21, 28 August, 5, 23, 22 September 1953); *Za pobedu*, 201 (Sarajevo 15. September 1953).
39 *Razvoj OS SFRJ*, vol. 3–1, 'Kopnena vojska'(VIZ Beograd 1988), pp. 87–88; Pejčić Predrag, *Čelična krila*, (Eksportpress Beograd 1985), p. 86; MJRV: RV i PVO: Operacijski dnevnik 32. lbad/14. mad; *Narodna armija*, 742, (Belgrade 27 September 1953).
40 Jović, Stojan , *Pod kupolom padobrana* (Narodna armija, Beograd 1980), 12; *Borba* (Belgrade, 26 September 1953), p.1; *Razvoj OS SFRJ*, vol. 3–1, pp. 87–88.
41 *Narodna armija*, 739, (Belgrade 17. septembar 1953); DAMSP: PA: f-44, 1953, 4, 412159.
42 DAMSP: PA: f-23, 9, 412306. Preparations for the Montgomery visit were carried out during the June and July. Marshal Tito agreed on the 15 June 1953 that the visit have "private" character. DAMSP, PA, str. pov, 1953, f-2, 486; DAMSP, f-23, 9, 412306; *Borba*, (Belgrade 29 August 1953 and 12, 16, 17, 19, 20, 26 September 1953).
43 *Za domovinu* 24, (Zagreb, 29 September 1953); *Borba*, (Belgrade 22, 24, 26 September 1953); *Narodna armija*. 741 (Belgrade 24 September 1953).
44 *Borba*, (Belgrade 26 September 1953), p. 1.
45 Tito, *Govori i članci*, vol. 8, pp. 237–239.
46 AJ: f. 112: reports: 97–98, 21. 9. 1953, 19,00 h; 22. 9 1953, 07,00 h; 23. 9. 1953, 11,00 h; 24. 9. 1953, 07,00 h, 19,00 h; 25. 9. 1953, 07,00 h, 19,00 h; 26. 9. 1953. 07,00 h, 19,00 h; 27. 9. 1953, 07,00 h; 29. 9 1953, 07,00 h; AJ 1036/1037, *Bilten prislušne službe Radio Jugoslavije 19. septembar 1953*; AJ 1062/1063, *specijalni informativni bilteni*; 17, 18, 19, 20, 21, 24, 25, 26 September 1953; *Borba*, (Belgrade 28 September 1953).
47 *Narodna armija* 742 and 743 (27, 30 Septembar 1953). AJ: f. 112: reports 97–98, 21. 9. 1953, 19,00 h; 22. 9. 1953, 07,00 h; 23. 9. 1953, 11,00 h; 24. 9. 1953, 07,00 h, 19,00 h; 25. 9. 1953, 07,00 h, 19,00 h; 26. 9. 1953. 07,00 h, 19,00 h; 27. 9. 1953, 07,00 h; 29. 9. 1953, 07,00 h; AJ 1036/1037, AJ 1062/1063.

Chapter 4

1 Novak, *Trieste 1941–1954*, p .430.
2 Novak, *Trieste 1941–1954*, p. 430.
3 Bekić, *Jugoslavija u Hladnom ratu*, pp.546-547.
4 Tito, *Govori i članci*, vol. 8, p. 321.
5 Istituto Luce Cinecittà, *Il problema di Trieste*. (https://www.youtube.com/watch?v=ytT1cd2FcTg&feature=youtu.be)
6 Bekić, *Jugoslavija u Hladnom ratu*, p. 547.
7 *Razvoj OS SFRJ*, vol. 3–2, p. 173; *Razvoj OS SFRJ*, vol. 13, p. 260.
8 See Appendix III; *Razvoj OS SFRJ*, vol. 5, p. 50 and appendix 7.
9 *Razvoj OS SFRJ*, vol. 5, p. 50; *Jugoslovenski mornar*, 11–1953 and 12–1953 (Split 1953); *Čuvar Jadrana*, 266, (Split 16 October 1953).
10 *Razvoj OS SFRJ*, vol. 5, 50; Order of battle of the JNA forces upon the: UO-MoD: 'Naredba DSNO pov. br. 830/52' and further changes noted up to October 1953.
11 Trifunović, Duško, 'Tukaj smo Slovenci!' *Komunist*, (Belgrade 22 July 1988), p. 24.
12 *Razvoj OS SFRJ*, vol. 3–2, p. 173.
13 Author's interview with ret. General Milosav Đorđević, Belgrade, 15 February 2000.
14 *Razvoj OS SFRJ*, vol. 5, p. 50.
15 *Borba*, (Belgrade, 10 October 1953).
16 *Razvoj OS SFRJ*, vol. 13, p. 260.
17 DAMSP, 1953, f-39, 24, 416350; *Razvoj OS SFRJ*, vol. 13, pp 262-263.
18 *Borba*, (Belgrade, 11 Oktober 1953).
19 Author's interview with ret. Colonel Nikolaj Marčesku , Belgrade, 21 December 1999/14 March 2000.
20 AJ: f. 112: reports: 99–100, 12. 10. 1953, 07,00 h, 15.00, 19,00 h; 13. 10. 1953 07,00 h, 18,00, 21,00 h, 14. 10. 1953, 07,00 h, 15,00 h; 15. 10. 1953, 07,00 h; 16. 10. 1953, 07,00 h, 19,00 h.
21 AJ: 112: reports 99–100, 11 October 1953, 07,00 h.
22 Jakšić, Pavle, *Nad uspomenama*, second volume, (Rad, Beograd 1990) pp. 112–113. General Đorđević, at that time a second lieutenant, remembered that while he was conducting the exercises with his soliders around Divaca (the last railway junction on the Yugoslav side prior to Trieste) he heard the characteristic noise of engines and tracks. Sudennly a column of T-34 tanks appeared, commanded by a certain Major Timosenko. It was the sprearhead of the 252th Tank Brigade heading towards the border just above Trieste. Author's interview with ret. General Milosav Đorđević, Belgrade, 15 February 2000.
23 Đilas, Milovan, *Druženje s Titom*, (Izdavači Milovan Đilas i Momčilo Đorgović Beograd 1990), p. 77.
24 *Za domovinu*, 27 (31 October 1953); *Borba*, (Belgrade 11, 14, 15 October 1953); *Narodna armija*, 745, (Belgrade 15 October 1953).
25 *Borba*, (Belgrade 11, 12, 13 October 1953); *Narodna armija*, 745, 746, (15, 22 October 1953).
26 AJ, f. 112, 99–100, 17 October 1953, 07,00 h.
27 MJRV: RV i PVO: 'Operacijski dnevnik 32. lbad/14. mad'.

28 *Razvoj OS SFRJ*, knj. 5, p. 50.
29 On the 1 January 1954, the III Air Corps had 272 aircraft on strength, among them 58 non serviceable. They equipped a total of three air divisions comprised of 10 aviation regiments, one training and one float-plane squadron.
30 VA: fond JNA: 5384/1977, *Pregled operativnog bojnog stanja posada i aviona sa resursima JRV u 1953. godini* with additional author research.
31 MJRV: RV i PVO: 'Operacijski dnevnik 32. lbad/14. mad', 9 October 1953 and onward.
32 Dimitrijević - Petrović , *Tanderbolt*, p. 6; Author's interview with ret. Lt Col Ljubomir Krstić at the time with 96th Aviation Regiment, Novi Beograd, December 1989; Author's interview with ret. Sgt Ilija Kračunov, who had served with the 83rd Aviation Regiment, Belgrade, August 1986.
33 MJRV: RV i PVO: k. 6–1, 'Referat za istoriju 21. mešovite avio-divizije (1949–1956)'; Micevski-Dimitrijevic, *83. lovacki puk*, 40-41.
34 MJRV: RV i PVO: 'Operacijski dnevnik 32. lbad/14. mad.'
35 Bošković, Rajica, *Nebo na dlanu - Vek vazdušnog osmtranja, javljanja i navođenja*, (autorsko izdanje, Beograd 2017. 104.
36 *Italian Air Force, 1945–1978*, pp. 56–61.
37 VA: fond JNA: 5384/1977, *Pregled operativnog bojnog stanja posada iaviona sa resursima JRV u 1953. godini*.
38 MJRV: RV i PVO: 'Operacijski dnevnik 32. lbad/14. mad.'
39 Author's interviews with ret. Lt Col Ljubomir Krstić and ret. Sgt Ilija Kračunov.
40 Author's interview with ret. Col. Predrag Vulic, at that time pilot with the 117th Aviation Regiment, Novi Beograd, October 2015.
41 MJRV: RV i PVO: 'Operacijski dnevnik 32. lbad/14. mad.'
42 Whole passage based on the article: Cappellano, *L' „esigenza T (Trieste)"*, pp. 18-23.
43 *Razvoj OS SFRJ*, vol. 13, pp. 260.
44 *Razvoj OS SFRJ*, vol. 13, pp. 260-262.
45 *Narodna armija,* 745, 747 (Belgrade 15, 29 October 1953); *Borba,* (Belgrade 29 October 1953).
46 Cappellano, *L' „esigenza T (Trieste)"*, pp. 22-23.
47 *Narodna armija,* 745, 747, 748, (Belgrade 15, 29 October, 5 November 1953); *Borba,* (Belgrade 28 October 1953); *Čuvar Jadrana,* 269, (Split, 6 November 1953).
48 Cappellano, *L' „esigenza T (Trieste)"*, p. 23.
49 *Narodna armija*, 748, (5 Novembar 1953); MJRV: RV i PVO: 'Operacijski dnevnik 32. lbad/14. mad.'
50 Author's interview with ret. General Nikola Zutic, Novi Beograd, September 1993.
51 Cappellano, *L' „esigenza T (Trieste)"*, p. 23.
52 *Zapisi i komentari, O školovanju i životu II klase Vojnopomorske akademija Jugoslovenske ratne mornarice* (Beograd 2008), 185, 193.
53 "Memorial room" of the 172th Fighter-bomber Aviation Regiment, Golubovci Air Base: *Istorijat 172. lbap za 1953. godinu*. (author visited this facility on 25th December 1989).
54 Author's interview with ret. Colonel Mitar Mitrović July 1990 at Novi Beograd.
55 MJRV: RV i PVO: 'Operacijski dnevnik 32. lbad/14. mad.'; Micevski and Dimitrijevic, *Balkan Mosquitos*, 30–32; *Istorijat 172. lbap za 1953. godinu.*
56 MJRV: RV i PVO: 'Operacijski dnevnik 32. lbad/14. mad.'
57 Sinobad, Milos, *103.izvidjacki avijacijski puk*, (Milos Sinobad, Beograd 2008), pp. 49-52.
58 Likso Tihomir, *Letačka karijera Miljenka Lipovšćaka 1939–1980* (D. Canak Nova Gradiška 2000), p.53.
59 MJRV: RV i PVO: 'Operacijski dnevnik 32. lbad/14. mad.'; *Razvoj OS SFRJ*, vol. 13, p. 261; Authors interviewed several retired members of the 103rd and 184th Recce Aviation Regiments in Belgrade and Nivi Beograd, September 1993: General Nikola Žutić, and Colonels Miloš Sinobad, Ivan Katić, Bogdan Kolničar and Marko Flajs.
60 Cappellano, *L' „esigenza T (Trieste)"*, p. 23.
61 DAMSP: PA: 1953, f-41, 3, 416881.
62 MJRV: RV i PVO: 'Operacijski dnevnik 32. lbad/14. mad.'; DAMSP: PA: 1953, f-41, 3, 416881 and 417000.
63 DAMSP: PA: 1953, f-41, 3, 416881 and 417000.
64 Roganović Mirko, '30 godina jedinica VOJIN', *Glasnik RV i PVO*, 3/83, (Beograd 1983), 8; AJ: f. 112: 99–100, 13 October 1953, 18,00 h; *Borba,* (Belgrade 22 October 1953); MJRV: RV i PVO: 'Operacijski dnevnik 32. lbad/14. mad.'; *Za domovinu*, 29, (Zagreb, 14 November 1953).
65 DAMSP: PA: 1953, 79, 5.
66 *Borba* (Belgrade, 9 October 1953); AJ: f. 112: 99–100, reports: 99–100, 12. 10. 1953, 07,00, 21,00 h; 14. 10. 1953, 19,00 h.
67 AJ: f. 112: 99–100, reports: 12. 10. 1953, 07,00, 21,00 h; 14. 10. 1953, 19,00 h, 15. 10. 1953, 07,00 h; 17. 10. 1953, 18,00 h.
68 *Borba,* (Belgrade 27 October 1953).
69 AJ: f. 112: 99–100, reports: 11. 10. 1953, 19,00 h , 12. 10. 1953, 07,00, 18,00 h
70 *Jugoslovenski mornar,* 11–1953 (Split 1953); *Borba,* (Belgrade, 10 October 1953). AJ: f. 112: 99–100, reports: 11. 10. 1953, 07,00 h and 15. 10. 1953, 07,00 h. *Čuvar Jadrana*, 267, (Split 23 October 1953).
71 Tito, *Govori i članci*, vol. 8, pp. 323–324.
72 AJ: f. 112: 99–100, reports:12. 10. 1953, 07,00 h; 14. 10. 1953, 07,00 h, 21,00 h.
73 Tito, *Govori i članci*, vol. 8, pp. 270–274, 290.
74 AJ: f. 112: 99–100, reports: 15. 10. 1953, 21,00 h; DAMSP: PA: str. pov. 1953, f-4, 529, I-417.
75 *Borba*, (Belgrade 4 November 1953).
76 Bekić, *Jugoslavija u Hladnom ratu,* p. 549.
77 Tito, *Govori i članci*, vol. 8, pp. 308.
78 Tito, *Govori i članci*, vol. 8, pp. 330–331; *Borba*, (Belgrade 24 October 1953).
79 Đilas, *Druzenje sa Titom*, 77.

Chapter 5

1 DAMSP, PA str. pov. 1953, f-4.
2 *Narodna armija*, 748, (Belgrade 5 November 1953), 1; *Titova reč u publikacijama JNA 1941–1980*, (VIZ, Beograd 1982), p.421.
3 Bekić, *Jugoslavija u Hladnom ratu,* pp. 560–561.
4 Tito, *Govori i članci*, vol. 8, pp.413.
5 MJRV: RV i PVO: 'Operacijski dnevnik 32. lbad/14. mad.'
6 British Pathe: *Trieste Riots (1953)* <https://www.youtube.com/watch?v=Mq56rmo5qtQ>; *Selected Originals - Trieste Riots (1953)* <https://www.youtube.com/watch?v=hEyC4ADqSF0>.
7 Bekić, *Jugoslavija u Hladnom ratu,* pp. 558.
8 *Čuvar Jadrana*, 271, (Split, 20 November 1953).
9 Bekić, *Jugoslavija u Hladnom ratu,* pp. 562–564; DAMSP, 1953, f-39, 32; *Narodna armija*, 753, (Belgrade 10 December 1953), *Borba,* (Belgrade 8, 9 and 12 December 1953).
10 Cappellano, *L' „esigenza T (Trieste)"*, p. 23.
11 *Borba,* (Belgrade 8, 9 and 12 December 1953); Author's interview with ret. General Milosav Đorđević; MJRV: RV i PVO: 'Operacijski dnevnik 32. lbad/14. mad.'
12 *Razvoj OS SFRJ*, vol. 5, 50; Author's interview with ret. General Milosav Đorđević.
13 Author's interview with ret. Colonel Petar Petković, at that time assigned to the 109th Aviation Regiment, Belgrade, 25 May 1998,
14 MJRV: RV i PVO: *Referat za istoriju 21. mad 1949–1956*, Author's interview with ret. Sgt Ilija Kračunov
15 Bekić, *Jugoslavija u Hladnom ratu,* p. 543.
16 Dimitrijević Bojan, 'The Mutual Defense Aid Program in Tito's Yugoslavia, 1951–1958 and its Technical Impact' (Edited by David M. Glantz), *The Journal of Slavic Military studies* vol. 10, no. 2, June 1997, (London 1997), pp. 19–33.
17 DAMSP, PA, str. pov., 1954. f-2, 1/114.
18 DAMSP, PA; str. pov, 1954, f-2, 238, 242, 313 and f-3 226.
19 DAMSP, PA; str. pov, 1954, f-2, 313.
20 DAMSP, PA, str. pov. 1954. f-2, I-1049.
21 British Pathe, *British Leave Trieste (1954),* <https://www.youtube.com/watch?v=ix8q0H_IlJU&feature=youtu.be>
22 *Trieste United States Troops,* <https://en.wikipedia.org/wiki/Trieste_United_States_Troops> (accessed 26 August 2108).
23 Novak, *Trieste 1941–1954,* p. 466.
24 *L'Esercito Italiano nel 1954* , http://nuovadifesa.altervista.org/lesercito-italiano-nel-1954/?doing_wp_cron=1534358667.3250820636749267578125 (accessed on 16 August 2018).
25 Novak, *Trieste 1941–1954,* p. 467.
26 *Ottobre 1954 - L' arrivo dei reparti dell' Esercito Italiano a Trieste nel giorno del ritorno della citta all' Italia* <https://archivioirredentista.wordpress.com/2014/10/24/26-ottobre-1954-larrivo-dei-reparti-dellesercito-italiano-a-trieste-nel-giorno-del-ritorno-della-citta-allitalia/> (accessed 15 August 2018).
27 British Pathe, *Trieste Is Returned To Italy (1954)* <https://www.youtube.com/watch?v=a9GrLiJPXvI>; *1954 il ritorno di Trieste all'Italia* <https://www.youtube.com/watch?v=QZoSySPPQ1s>; Istituto Luce Cinecittà, *La liberazione di Trieste: l'arrivo delle truppe italiane in città (1954)* https://www.youtube.com/watch?v=Np4KYdQyWM0>; Istituto Luce Cinecittà, *26 ottobre 1954, ritorno di Trieste all'Italia* (https://www.youtube.com/watch?v=VLR0EHFuUGg).
28 Ministarstvo odbrane Republike Srbije, *Medija centar Odbrana*, black and white film roles: 1954_LBW_ 00273-00276.
29 Novak, *Trieste 1941–1954,* 468.
30 BETFOR, *The Intelligence Corps in Venezia Giulia 1945 - 1954,* <http://betforassociation.org/BETFORTSO.html>, (accessed 26 August 2018).
31 AJ: f. 187 *Savezna uprava za investicije i izgradnju*: 2–10; *Razvoj OS SFRJ*, vol. 3–2, pp. 153 and 174; *Razvoj OS SFRJ*, vol. 13, p. 121.
32 VA: JNA: k.20, f.1, 2 'Operativni izvestaj za 1954/55 godinu'; UO-MoD, *Naredba DSNO pov. br. 830/52 sa upisanim promenama.*
33 VA: JNA: k.19, f.2, 2 'Operativni izvestaj za 1953/54 godinu'.
34 *Razvoj OS SFRJ,* vol. 3–2, p. 173.
35 *Razvoj OS SFRJ,* vol. 3–2, p. 50. The cadets of the class which had finished their courses at the beginning of September 1953 remained in the School in Vipava, until 1 October 1953. Author's interview with Milan Draskovic who was a cadet at the time, Novi Beograd, July 1998.
36 *Razvoj OS SFRJ*, vol. 23, 'Muzička služba', Beograd 1987, p. 110.
37 Šantić Sreten, 'Viša vazduhoplovna oficirska škola' in *Čuvari našeg neba,* Beograd 1977, pp. 300–302.
38 *Razvoj OS SFRJ,* vol. 5, p. 51.
39 *Razvoj OS SFRJ,* vol. 5, p. 51.
40 MJRV: RV i PVO: 'Operacijski dnevnik 32. lbad/14. mad.'
41 *Razvoj OS SFRJ,* vol. 13, pp. 262–264.
42 Cappellano, *L' „esigenza T (Trieste)"*, p.22-23.
43 Cappellano, *L' „esigenza T (Trieste)"*, p.22-23.

ACKNOWLEDGMENTS

The author would like to use this opportunity to thank: colleagues in the Belgrade-based Military Archive and Military Museum for their assistance with this work, but especially to the officers of the Department for Organisation, Ministry of Defence and to the helpful gentlemen that have worked in the Medija Centar Odbrana photo archive: Radovan Popović and Zoran Milovanović. I would also like to express gratitude to a number of veterans interviewed upon this matter in previous years.

Also, to friends who provided help with their photo collections: Milan Micevski, Aleksandar Smiljanić (Serbia), Tomaž Perme (Slovenia), Mario Raguž and David Orlović (Croatia), to Zvonimir Despot (Croatia) for additional help and Miroslav Šljivić (Serbia) who recommended the author to Helion & Co Publishing.

Finally, the author wishes to thank Tom Cooper and Duncan Rogers for their confidence to accept this exotic military history subject for their prestigious Europe@War series.

ABOUT THE AUTHOR

Bojan Dimitrijević works as a historian and is the Deputy Director of the Institute for Contemporary History, Belgrade, Serbia. Educated at the Universities of Belgrade and Novi Sad, CEU Budapest and University of Bradford, and has worked as the custodian of the Yugoslav Aviation Museum.

During the period 2003-2009, Dimitrijevic served as advisor to the Minister of Defence, the Minister of Foreign Affairs, the President of Serbia, and as Assistant to the Minister of Defence. He has published over 50 different books and more than 100 scientific articles in Serbia and abroad. His professional interest is in the military history of the former Yugoslavia and Balkans in World War Two and the Cold War, as well as the wars in the 1990s. This is his first instalment for Helion.